THE DEVIL
SHALL
NOT PREVAIL

Books by A.W. Tozer

Compiled and Edited by James L. Snyder

Alive in the Spirit

And He Dwelt Among Us

Authentic Worship

A Cloud by Day, a Fire by Night

The Crucified Life

The Dangers of a Shallow Faith

Delighting in God

The Devil Shall Not Prevail

A Disruptive Faith

The Essential Tozer Collection 3-in-1

Experiencing the Presence of God

The Fire of God's Presence

God's Power for Your Life

Going Higher with God in Prayer

Lead like Christ

Living as a Christian

My Daily Pursuit

No Greater Love

Preparing for Jesus' Return

The Purpose of Man

The Pursuit of God

The Quotable Tozer

Reclaiming Christianity

Voice of a Prophet

The Wisdom of God

Books by James L. Snyder

The Life of A.W. Tozer: In Pursuit of God—The Authorized Biography

THE DEVIL SHALL NOT PREVAIL

UNSHAKABLE CONFIDENCE IN GOD'S ALMIGHTY POWER

A.W. TOZER

COMPILED AND EDITED BY JAMES L. SNYDER

BETHANYHOUSE
a division of Baker Publishing Group
Minneapolis, Minnesota

© 2023 by James L. Snyder

Published by Bethany House Publishers
Minneapolis, Minnesota
www.bethanyhouse.com

Bethany House Publishers is a division of
Baker Publishing Group, Grand Rapids, Michigan

Printed in the United States of America

ISBN 9780764240294 (paperback)
ISBN 9780764242274 (casebound)
ISBN 9781493443796 (ebook)

Library of Congress Cataloging-in-Publication Control Number: 2023031466

Unless otherwise indicated, Scripture quotations are from the New King James Version®. Copyright © 1982 by Thomas Nelson. Used by permission. All rights reserved.

Scripture quotations labeled KJV are from the King James Version of the Bible.

James L. Snyder is represented by The Steve Laube Agency.

Baker Publishing Group publications use paper produced from sustainable forestry practices and post-consumer waste whenever possible.

23 24 25 26 27 28 29   7 6 5 4 3 2 1

CONTENTS

INTRODUCTION

A.W. Tozer was very passionate about worship. This came before anything else, and whatever interfered with his worship, he dealt with as firmly as possible. One of the things interfering with that worship was the devil.

Tozer often said he would rather talk about anything other than the devil. He never wanted to give the devil any credit, but because the devil poses a significant threat in undermining our worship, he must be dealt with. This book is not based on a series of sermons on the devil, but on selected sermons focusing on the devil's influence on the life of the Christian and how we can better protect ourselves from evil.

Tozer often referred to Ephesians 6:10–11, where the apostle Paul wrote, "Finally, my brethren, be strong in the Lord and in the power of His might. Put on the whole armor of God, that you may be able to stand against the wiles of the devil." It is the standing against the "wiles of the devil" that Tozer emphasizes in this book. And to stand against the devil, we need to be prepared spiritually. Many of the chapters involve building ourselves up in the Lord, so we are in a position to resist the devil's temptations.

Tozer rejected the world's definition of the devil, as well as Hollywood's, since they both have characterized him in ways that are not compliant with the Word of God. What, then, does the Bible have to teach us about the devil? For *that* is what we need to remember.

Even though Tozer didn't like discussing the devil, he stressed that we as believers should never take him for granted. Many people assume they can defeat the devil in his own territory, i.e., this world in which we live, and that the devil isn't much more than a menacing presence. Biblically speaking, this is not the case. Instead, we must view the devil as an enemy of God and therefore the enemy of our souls.

In practicing spiritual warfare, there are several truths we need to be aware of. First, we must come to understand who exactly the enemy is. Too many Christians have no idea who the real enemy is and instead point their fingers at someone at church or someone in their family or perhaps workplace. Yet to wage battle against the enemy, we need to learn who he is, and it's only in God's Word that we get a clear understanding of him.

In the fourth chapter of Matthew, we see Jesus going up against the devil head on. The interesting thing about this passage of Scripture is that Jesus didn't take the devil for granted. We see Jesus approaching the enemy of God through the quoting of Scripture, always responding to the devil's attacks by saying, "It is written."

While knowing your enemy is vital to developing a strategy against him, another aspect has to do with understanding our spiritual warfare equipment. "Put on the whole armor of God, that you may be able to stand against the wiles of the devil." If we don't have the whole armor of God, we will not stand for long. The devil only requires a small vulnerable spot in which to focus his attack.

A large portion of this book involves preparing ourselves to encounter the enemy wherever that may occur, guarding against those things that might compromise our ability to stand against him, and confronting him from God's perspective—the way Jesus did when being tempted in the wilderness.

Tozer was concerned about our spiritual growth as Christians, so that the devil could not make inroads and manipulate our hearts and minds. He makes it clear that the devil cannot take away our salvation; however, he can hinder our Christian life and cause us to forfeit our reward when someday we meet the Lord in heaven. If the devil cannot take away your salvation, he'll do everything he can to steal your joy plus any fruit you may have received as a follower of Christ.

This book is meant to show how critical it is that we understand our vulnerability toward the devil's wiles. We cannot deal with him in our own strength, that much is certain. And the key element of the devil's attacks against believers is to undermine their confidence in God.

Tozer points out that this confidence is not based on our understanding of the situation before us. He often repeated Paul's words, "For we walk by faith, not by sight" (2 Corinthians 5:7). That is to say, we trust God in situations that we cannot understand from a human standpoint. If the devil can get us to question our confidence in God, he'll have us pointed in the wrong direction.

To stand against the enemy, we need to be everything God wants us to be and have all that God wants us to have in this battle. It's possible we will not know every battle before us, for that too is one of the strategies of the enemy. But if we can trust God wholeheartedly even when we don't understand our situation or circumstances, with God's help we'll defeat the devil every time.

Dr. James L. Snyder

—1—

FACING OUR REAL ENEMY

Then David said to the Philistine, "You come to me with a
sword, with a spear, and with a javelin. But I come to you
in the name of the LORD of hosts, the God of the armies of
Israel, whom you have defied."

1 Samuel 17:45

Every battle begins with understanding who the enemy is. If
soldiers do not know who the enemy is, how then are they
going to be prepared to deal with them? I believe a lot of
Christians today do not know their real enemy. The enemy
is not in the church pews. Many Christians spend a lot of
time in conflict with one another, much to the great delight
of our enemy the devil.

It's in our understanding of the enemy that we can begin
to prepare ourselves for the battle and ongoing conflict that
is before us. As Christians, we are engaged in what is called

spiritual warfare, and this war cannot be fought with physical or military might, guns, and torpedoes. How we comprehend spiritual warfare says a lot about our relationship with Christ. Many do not realize the significance of the spiritual fight we are in and the fact that this very real enemy has marked each of us for attack.

The apostle Paul set forth our responsibility when it comes to spiritual warfare: "Finally, my brethren, be strong in the Lord and in the power of His might. Put on the whole armor of God, that you may be able to stand against the wiles of the devil" (Ephesians 6:10–11).

One of the great Old Testament stories is the story of David and Goliath. Goliath represented the latest technology in military warfare. He was a man of prowess and strength, had the best equipment, and was well trained for battle. His whole life had been devoted to fighting and vanquishing the enemy, and he was confident that he could defeat anyone.

David, on the other side of the field, was a young man who had no experience or training whatsoever in battle. When he faced Goliath, it was not a fair match from a human standpoint.

When David was given his first slingshot, I'm sure he didn't look at it and think, *This slingshot will help me take down Goliath, the enemy of Israel.* As a young man, David had never heard of Goliath, and he likely didn't comprehend the danger Israel was facing. In other words, we never know what or who God will use for His purposes, nor when or how. When we place ourselves in God's hands in submission and obedience, we are at His disposal, and He always prepares us for the battle in front of us. That is why it is crucial that we learn how to wait on the Lord.

So David was inexperienced when it came to warfare and fighting techniques, not knowing how to triumph on the battlefield. He was simply a shepherd boy who was naive concerning the greater world. His expertise lay in taking care of his family's sheep out in the fields. He knew how to deal with the wolves and the bears, but outside of that, he had no experience.

As David went before Goliath, he told the Philistine, "You come to me with a sword, with a spear, and with a javelin. But I come to you in the name of the LORD of hosts, the God of the armies of Israel, whom you have defied" (1 Samuel 17:45). Prior to this encounter with Goliath, King Saul thought it was his responsibility to prepare and equip David for the battle. "Then David said to Saul, 'Let no man's heart fail because of him; your servant will go and fight with this Philistine.' And Saul said to David, 'You are not able to go against this Philistine to fight with him; for you are a youth, and he a man of war from his youth'" (1 Samuel 17:32–33).

This was David's testimony before King Saul. Why King Saul went along with this little boy named David is beyond my understanding.

"So Saul clothed David with his armor, and he put a bronze helmet on his head; he also clothed him with a coat of mail. David fastened his sword to his armor and tried to walk, for he had not tested them. And David said to Saul, 'I cannot walk with these, for I have not tested them.' So David took them off" (1 Samuel 17:38–39).

David had no hesitancy in believing that God was on his side. His confidence was rooted in his lifelong relationship with Yahweh or Jehovah, as God was called then. Thus David's strength and confidence was not in knowing everything

13

about the enemy, but in understanding and knowing his re-lationship with God.

To study the life of David is to delve deeply into his confidence in God. No doubt he did a lot of things that were wrong, but when everything was on the table, his confidence in God was unshaken.

The end of the story, of course, is that David came out victorious, while the enemy of Israel was defeated.

There is also the confrontation David had with Nathan the prophet concerning the episode with Bathsheba and her husband, whom David had killed. When Nathan rebuked David, saying, "You are the man!" (2 Samuel 12:7), David did not do what Nathan was afraid he would do. As king, David could have ordered that Nathan be executed, but he did no such thing. Instead, he fell on his knees in utter repentance, which I'm sure surprised Nathan.

David's repentance before God reveals the confidence that he had in God even when he failed and things went terribly wrong. For anybody to have such confidence in God in David's situation is beyond human comprehension. His confidence was bigger than his failure.

On the day David faced off with Goliath, he was not doing so because he felt confident in his own strength and ability and understanding; he faced off with Goliath solely because of his confidence in his God.

Scripture tells us that David had no confidence in King Saul or in the equipment Saul had for him. Rather, David turned his back on everything and everybody and fought Goliath simply because he knew what God could do.

It's important for Christians to cultivate the same sort of confidence in God that we see exhibited by David throughout his life. For it was this confidence that made him fearless, a man of faith. Many have tried to introduce into the Church the equipment and technology and methods that come from the world, but attempts like this have no place in the Church. We must embrace confidence in God to do what God has called us to do the way God wants it done.

But what does it mean to have confidence in God? Often we are tempted to use the world's definition of the word *confidence* instead of relying on God's definition. Paul said, "For we walk by faith, not by sight" (2 Corinthians 5:7). At the center of our confidence in God is our faith and trust in Him for all things—regardless of whether we understand the situation before us at the time.

Paul also said, "So then faith comes by hearing, and hearing by the word of God" (Romans 10:17). Our faith, then, is grounded and nourished in the Word of God. As we surrender ourselves to His Word, He begins to develop the faith in us that we need to have His perspective, which in turn nourishes our confidence in Him.

The world offers a lot of things that we can choose to place our faith in. Everybody puts their faith in something or someone. For the Christian, that faith is the result of the illuminating power of the Holy Spirit in our lives. We come to the Word of God not as experts but as passionate worshipers of God. The Bible is not a "beat the chest" kind of thing, but rather it enables us to worship God as He desires and deserves to be worshiped.

Our confidence is a result of the passionate worship that God has created within our hearts. It has nothing to do with knowledge or experience or technology. It has everything to do with the inward working of the Holy Spirit in our lives.

The Scriptures give no indication that David ever bragged about his experience with Goliath. He never tried to tell people what a brave person he was when he took on that great giant and defeated him.

If we have true confidence in God, we do not need personal affirmations. We must surrender that completely to God because our battles are not based on any battles we had previously, which often seems to be how people think. What we need to understand is that every battle is unique in and of itself. The main thing each battle does is confirm our confidence in God.

The roots of self-confidence are in the devil himself. It was the devil who said, "I will be like the Most High" (Isaiah 14:14). This attitude of self-confidence has been transferred to humanity. We now have confidence that we can overcome anything. If we can think it, we can achieve it.

That may work in the fantastical world of entertainment, but it does not work in the spiritual world of being confident in God and living confidently in Him. Self-confidence takes all the glory away from God and brings it back to us. If we have confidence in ourselves, we will fail at spiritual warfare.

"Put on the whole armor of God . . ." (Ephesians 6:11). By that, Paul meant that we need to take on everything of God and shun the flesh. You cannot have the armor of God and indulge the flesh. The enemy would have us concentrate on the flesh, protect the flesh, and put our confidence in the flesh. However, when we do that, we rob God of that which rightfully belongs to Him.

"I come to you in the name of the LORD of hosts, the God of the armies of Israel, whom you have defied," David said to Goliath.

In spiritual warfare, we find that God does things that are beyond human understanding. Therefore, we must stop second-guessing God.

When the Israelites were being led by Moses out of Egypt, they got only so far before coming to the Red Sea. They were angry with Moses and blamed him for their failure. In Exodus 14:10–12, we read of their approaching the Red Sea, with the Egyptian army not far behind them. They had no solution to the problem facing them—no human solution, that is. It is a great delight for God to bring His people to a place with no human solution at their disposal. When we come to that place, God will show us how powerful He is.

At the very last moment, God parted the Red Sea for the children of Israel, and they marched between the walls of water, heading for the Promised Land. The part that's most interesting about this story is that as soon as the children of Israel got across the Red Sea and reached the other side, the Egyptian army, running hard behind them, entered the Red Sea in pursuit. God brought the sea back together and the whole of the army of Egypt was destroyed in that moment.

Sometimes God brings us to a place where we don't know how to deal with the enemy, but the enemy soon finds it is God whom they're fighting. I think of Joseph in the Old Testament, a young man who encountered many problems and difficulties, none of them of his own making. It started with his brothers selling him into slavery and eventually led to his imprisonment in Egypt. Then, as the story goes, God brought Joseph out of slavery, and he was made second only to Pharaoh himself. He then went on to save the people of that time from a devastating famine that threatened them.

When the famine grew worse, Pharaoh allowed Joseph to bring his family to Egypt, and this was how Israel got to be in that land. Yet after his father died, Joseph's brothers were very much alarmed. They thought now that their father was dead, Joseph would seek revenge and repay them for their evil deeds aimed at their brother Joseph.

I like what Joseph told them: "But as for you, you meant evil against me; but God meant it for good, in order to bring it about as it is this day, to save many people alive" (Genesis 50:20). Joseph endured much hardship and suffering to accomplish with God what he could never have imagined.

Joseph's confidence in God enabled God to use him without explaining what He was going to do. That's true confidence. Often we want God to explain everything before it happens so we can then give God our approval. Of course, God doesn't need our approval for anything.

Our confidence in God must be unconditional. God wants us to get to a place where He can accomplish His will far and above what I could ever comprehend or even put into words.

Someday when we get to heaven, I believe we will be surprised to see how God used us while we were here on earth. The trials and tribulations we have gone through may not make sense to us, but in heaven we will begin to understand how God was using each difficult situation in our lives to accomplish something we could not comprehend at the time. I think this is why James wrote, "My brethren, count it all joy when you fall into various trials" (James 1:2).

Such rejoicing is an act of faith. They might not make sense at the time, all the things that happen to us. Still, we can rejoice because our confidence in God is that He is actively using us in ways we can't understand right now and that, through us, God is defeating the enemy. Our confidence in God is worthy of Him even though we may not see what God is doing and how God is using us.

How did David know that he would slay Goliath in the name of the Lord? How did Joseph know during his agonizing journey that he'd end up precisely where God wanted him to bring blessing to all those around him?

Confidence in God releases us from the need to understand all that God is doing. Sometimes we don't realize that God was using us until after it's all over.

Dear Father in heaven, what a blessing it is to be used by You, even if I don't always know at the time that You're using me. May my heart be so surrendered to Thee, O God, that You can carry out Your perfect will through me for Your glory. In Jesus' name, amen.

A MIGHTY FORTRESS IS OUR GOD

A mighty fortress is our God,
a bulwark never failing;
our helper he, amid the flood
of mortal ills prevailing.
For still our ancient foe
does seek to work us woe;
his craft and power are great,
and armed with cruel hate,
on earth is not his equal.

Did we in our own strength confide,
our striving would be losing,

were not the right Man on our side,
the Man of God's own choosing.
You ask who that may be?
Christ Jesus, it is he;
Lord Sabaoth his name,
from age to age the same;
and he must win the battle.

And though this world, with devils filled,
should threaten to undo us,
we will not fear, for God has willed
his truth to triumph through us.
The prince of darkness grim,
we tremble not for him;
his rage we can endure,
for lo! his doom is sure;
one little word shall fell him.

That Word above all earthly powers
no thanks to them abideth;
the Spirit and the gifts are ours
through him who with us sideth.
Let goods and kindred go,
this mortal life also;
the body they may kill:
God's truth abideth still;
his kingdom is forever!

                              Martin Luther (1529)

—2—

THE DANGER
OF COMPROMISING
OUR CONFIDENCE

Catch us the foxes,
The little foxes that spoil the vines,
For our vines have tender grapes.

Song of Solomon 2:15

To defeat our enemy, we must not allow our confidence in God to be compromised. It seems that many times we are prepared for the big battles, but it is the small battles that end up defeating us. And by small battles I mean the battles that are unexpected.

Solomon understood this when he wrote about "little foxes." These little foxes were the tiny things, and almost anything seems benign when it's little. From all appearances they offer no threat. For example, a lion cub is a pretty thing; if little enough, I wouldn't mind petting it myself. Almost any creature, even a baby pig, is a lovely little thing—enjoyable to handle, cute and pleasant to look at, and nice to have around. But when the lion cub or piglet grows older and bigger, we don't feel the same way about them, do we?

It's the same with foxes. When they are small, their ears are bigger than the rest of their face. Their tails are out of proportion and awkward, yet so cuddly and cute that nobody ever thinks a little fox dangerous to have around. And yet these little foxes love nothing better than to eat the young grapes before they come out fully. The tendrils of the little bunch of grapes that lost their flowers begin to shape up, and the embryonic grape is so tender and juicy that a little fox can't help but run about and snatch up those little grapes. But once a bunch of grapes has been eaten, even though it was green and hadn't grown to maturity, that is the end of that particular bunch of grapes. They will never materialize.

There are little foxes in the Christian life as well, foxes that are not yet full-grown and that never received any attention from the evangelist or minister of the gospel. The clergy and leaders in the Church tend to focus on certain big ugly sins and beat them to death, but there are little foxes among them which are just as deadly to the vine. And our enemy knows how to manipulate these little foxes to his advantage.

Christians who overlook or ignore the little things are making a great mistake. The assumption is that such little things pose no real danger to us, and we can handle them. That plays directly into the enemy's strategy. Whatever threat to our spiritual health we choose to ignore, the enemy twists around so as to compromise our confidence in God.

Many will say, "I'm ready for the big battle." The problem is that we prepare more for the big things that could happen to us than the little things. Our confidence is emboldened when we are facing big problems, but it is the little problems that undermine our confidence in God.

Here are several little foxes that I believe the enemy uses to destroy the vines of our confidence in God:

SENSITIVENESS

Our being overly sensitive can be a hindrance in the Christian life. This is also true of the saints. I can imagine that the apostle Paul was highly sensitive in many regards. Sensitiveness is a good thing, but it carries the potential to invite trouble in the Christian life when it stems from being too easily hurt. It is dangerous to go around with a tiny Christian chip on your shoulder, ready to flare up if you're not given the right amount of respect. It's a hindrance and a little fox, and we may even pick it up and admire its big ears and all the rest. Yet it can spoil all the young grapes that are just beginning to grow. They'll never come to fruition because they have been killed in the bud by an oversensitive disposition.

We need to pray to God to deliver us if we are by disposition inclined to be oversensitive. There is only one way to prevent the little fox from destroying the vines, and that is to destroy the little fox. You can't argue with it, you can't reason with it, you can only exterminate it. Let's pray that the Lord will give us a certain toughness, the ability to endure and smile at the little insults and affronts that come our way. Let us instead have the mind of Christ in all things and in all our interactions with others.

DISLOYALTY

While loyalty is certainly a virtue, loyalty gone wrong can be deadly. Disloyalty is even more deadly than loyalty gone wrong. Of course, we ought to be loyal to something for our own soul's sake. And yet this modern age has led to flabby principles and lukewarm allegiances, which have adversely affected many Christians in our day. We must ask ourselves: To whom are we loyal? Where do our loyalties lie?

When the disciples walked with the Lord Jesus, they formed a tight circle of loyalty. What was so wonderful with that circle was that when Jesus said, "One of you will betray Me," not one of them responded, "Judas Iscariot is the one who will betray Him." They had their arguments, and they did a lot of carnal things, but not one of them said, "Judas is the traitor." Instead, each of them replied, "Lord, is it I?" (Matthew 26:21–22). They were loyal even to Judas. When later Judas approached Jesus to kiss Him (Matthew 26:49), Jesus called him "friend" or "companion." So we can afford to cultivate our loyalties further. In our efforts to be broad and ecumenical, we should not forget that there is always a little circle of people to whom we should be loyal, and a message and a program to which we should be loyal.

LAZINESS

We must challenge each other to run from laziness. For Christians who are too lazy to read God's Word; too lazy to study it and pray; too lazy to meet their obligations, promising others they will do such things at a later time—that's a little fox, a cute little fellow who is nibbling the grapes.

I have found that praying, for instance, is a hard business. It's not something that comes easy. Prayer that comes easy is neither good nor effective. Praying should cost you something. But most of us are too lazy to pray, to seek Him with sincerity and humility, and we're too lazy to study His Word. Jesus, however, who is our model and the example to be followed, was tireless. Yes, our Lord was a tireless worker. He chose working men to be his disciples, not playboys and not men about town and not men rich enough to retire early. Our Lord chose working men, for He said, "My Father has been working until now, and I have been working" (John 5:17). So we must pray that we might be delivered from the little fox of laziness.

COMPLACENCY

We should be aware that too much contentment is one thing for the unredeemed person, but it's something else entirely for the Christian. In fact, it can prove deadly. Contentment judges ourselves by what we used to be, not what we ought to be. It says, "If I measure up to what I was, I will be all right." Let us rather say, "I'll measure up to what I ought to be."

It is our confidence in God that spurs us on to becoming everything God wants us to become. The only way we can know that is to get to know God personally and intimately. Confidence based on lectures or training has a very short limit.

Each day presents for us a challenge. If we don't look for the challenge, this is bound to undermine our confidence in

God. If we think for one minute that the Christian life is easy and that all we have to do is mumble a few words, practice a few rituals, and attend church whenever it's convenient, we will never gain the confidence we need to be what God wants us to be.

I think of Paul's urgent words about pushing oneself toward the goal: "Not that I have already attained, or am already perfected; but I press on, that I may lay hold of that for which Christ Jesus has also laid hold of me. . . . I press toward the goal for the prize of the upward call of God in Christ Jesus" (Philippians 3:12, 14).

When followers of Christ get up Sunday morning and go to church, they should hear the preacher tell them how far they will have to go before becoming as perfect as their Father in heaven is perfect. Not congratulating ourselves because of where we've come from, but rather urging ourselves further on. So let's be careful of complacency. Let's keep stirring ourselves up to "pursue righteousness, godliness, faith, love, patience, gentleness," and to "fight the good fight of faith" (1 Timothy 6:11–12).

SOFTNESS

The Bible says we need to endure hardship: "You therefore must endure hardship as a good soldier of Jesus Christ. No one engaged in warfare entangles himself with the affairs of this life, that he may please him who enlisted him as a soldier" (2 Timothy 2:3–4).

After the Second World War ended, the United States had a civilian army, which attempted to make army life much like home life. It wasn't long before the rigid discipline relaxed.

One of the higher-up officials of the army stated, "When the Korean War hit us, we found our new relaxed, easy attitude trying to make the army as much like home as possible and take all the hardness out of it. So we got captured and got sent to prison camps." He added, "Who died first? A soft voice died first." He went on to say that those boys who had gone through rigorous discipline and tough training were hard on themselves. To use his words, "The boys who went in soft died like flies." We can't have a civilian army. We must have a military army, people who learn to stand firm under all circumstances.

Let's watch out for *spiritual* softness that looks always for the easy way out—the way which trickles down over the hills of the kingdom of God like a lazy stream seeking the path of least resistance. We need in the Church today those who can endure hardship, persevering with their eyes fixed on Christ, who is our refuge.

SELF-PITY

Self-pity is a character weakness that says, "Poor me, I'm not appreciated." I feel this way at times, and I don't mind telling you that sometimes I sense that little fox scratching on my door. I find myself thinking, *I'm sure that my people don't appreciate me.* Then I smile and say, "Now there's that fox again." And I get rid of that nasty little fox as fast as I can.

Let us be careful, then, not to pity ourselves that we're unappreciated by others, but rather let us remember and then dwell on the Father's unfailing love for us, keeping this the focus of our hearts.

DISCOURAGEMENT

This is Satan's best act. When nothing else can stop a person from moving ahead in God's will, discouragement will do the trick every time. Take poor Elijah, for example. He wasn't afraid of the devil; after all, he'd faced four hundred prophets of Baal. Then suddenly he got discouraged, ran and hid in a cave, and under a juniper tree, in deep despair, he prayed to die. Though the Lord didn't let Elijah die, He never let him perform any worthy act after that. God whisked him off to heaven and said, "This man is too discouraged; he's no good anymore."

If we find ourselves discouraged, let us turn to Christ, the Light of the World, and place our dispirited lives in His hands, along with any feelings of hopelessness. Let us ask for His help in guiding us out of the darkness, casting all our care upon Him, for He cares for us (1 Peter 5:7), and keeping in mind Jesus' promise that we will find rest for our souls: "For My yoke is easy and My burden is light" (Matthew 11:29–30). Finally, let us turn to the fellowship of our brothers and sisters in the Lord.

Not one of these foxes I have mentioned is a full-sized fox, and yet they're just as destructive as if they were. These don't disgrace a Christian, and the Church tolerates such things. It not only tolerates them, but also uses and promotes people filled with them, resulting in tattered, ragged vines and little or no fruit.

Let us trust the blood of Jesus to sweep these little foxes out of our hearts and cleanse us from them completely. Let's eradicate them from our lives. We can trust the Lord to move in and deliver us from the foxes the enemy uses to destroy the vines of our confidence in Him.

Help me, Father, to recognize those little foxes that are causing damage in my life. Give me the courage to stand up against them, and help me, O God, to fight the good fight in the light of Your glory. I praise and honor You. Amen.

CHRIST LEADS ME ON

Christ leads me on to higher ground,
He shows the way to me,
Since I in Him salvation found,
I know He leadeth me.
He leads me on,
I trust in Him,
His guiding hand I see,
His spirit walks with me each day,
I know He leadeth me.

Christ leads me on to broader fields,
A leader true is He,
Since I my soul to Him did yield,
I know He leadeth me.
He leads me on,
I trust in Him,
His guiding hand I see,
His spirit walks with me each day,
I know He leadeth me.

Christ leads me on tho' ways be rough,
And dark the paths may be,

I trust in Him for grace enough,
I know He leadeth me.
He leads me on,
I trust in Him,
His guiding hand I see,
His spirit walks with me each day,
I know He leadeth me.

E. M. Bartlett (1922)

—3—

Causes of Backsliding, the Devil's Toolbox

The backslider in heart will be filled with his own ways, but a good man will be satisfied from above.

Proverbs 14:14

I'd rather write on any number of subjects I can think of other than the issue of backsliding. But it is age-old and universal, and the Bible has much to say about it. Therefore, I think it right and proper that I should lay before you something of what the Bible tells us, both a warning and a word of encouragement about backsliding. It is a weapon the devil uses most successfully.

I believe the word *backsliding* came from the backward slide mentioned in the book of Hosea: "For Israel slideth back as a backsliding heifer: now the LORD will feed them as a lamb in a large place" (Hosea 4:16 KJV). The idea was—and I've seen this on the farm myself—an animal starts up a slippery bank and gets partway up, then loses control and traction, slips back, and only after many attempts do they make it up to the top. Sometimes they slide back and can't get up at all. Hosea, a man of God with no intention of being fictitious, said that Israel was like the animals he'd seen trying to climb a slippery hill after a heavy rain. So they went, worked hard at it, pushed, and then slid back as many steps as they had gone up.

One cause of backsliding is the fickleness of the human heart.

It would be wonderful if we could remain what we were, but it would also be a most damning thing. How sad our state by nature is, and if we could not change, we would be automatically doomed to remain in that sad state while the ages passed. Yet our ability to change our minds and to go from worse to better is our hope. The call of God in repentance is a call from worse to better.

If we could not go from one state to another, we would be frozen, morally static, and condemned from birth. But because we can move from one moral state to another, we can go from bad to good and can get right with God even though we were wrong before. We can become good, though we were bad before; we can become holy, though we were unholy before. Well, that same ability to move from one moral state to another and to change our minds about things can also cause backsliding.

One outcome of fickleness is that we switch from one interest to another. I've seen this with children. When tiny, they have one idea what it is they like. When nine or ten, they have another. And when in their midteens, they have yet another. Of course, this is true of adults as well. Fads change again and again, one style of dress or suit to another, shifting from one thing that interests us to another that interests us more. Such fickleness in people can also translate to the moral world.

The only behaviors we stick to as a rule are those that nature or circumstance has dictated we not deviate from, such as eating, drinking, and sleeping. So long as the human race lives on, there will always be a desire for food and to protect ourselves. These are instincts that reside deep in human nature. Furthermore, we tend to turn away from anything that requires attention and careful, painstaking labor.

Take a young pianist, for example. I wonder how many people have started piano lessons but didn't go through with learning to play the instrument. Like so many others, I didn't continue with my piano lessons when I was young. Why? Because mastering the piano is not an instinct with us. There was no instinctive impulse waking me at night and pushing me toward the piano. It just wasn't in me.

Musically speaking, certain people have something within them that almost amounts to an instinct. We refer to them as natural-born musicians. They exhibit some kind of musical expression and have no trouble with practicing an instrument for hours each day because doing so is in them. Still, this is the exception. The majority of people don't do what becomes arduous, irksome, and unpleasant to them. Conversely, we tend to follow the easy way, and outside of taxes and certain other duties that are forced upon us from the outside, either by nature or by law, by and large we do what we like to do—that which comes naturally to us.

And of course that is the fertile soil in which backsliding grows.

Many people, perhaps due to some great pressure, fear, loss, and bereavement, turn to God and make promises. But the instinct to follow through, to follow *Him*, is not in them. Their instinct, in fact, pushes them the other way. Before long, reading and studying the Bible and praying becomes painstaking and feels unnatural. And so we turn back to our former ways a little at a time as the days pass.

If we had every person in the nation stand, who at some point made a step toward God to follow His ways, but who had since forgotten all about it and are now living as if there were no God in heaven above, I tell you, it would be a shock. We wouldn't get over it if we could see them all standing like soldiers lined up. We'd be horrified by how many had made this step toward God, maybe even met God in a personal way, but because serving Jesus Christ was contrary to their nature, they turned away.

If people had remained what they originally were, made in the image of God without sin, then it would be perfectly natural to serve God. The angels in heaven above and the seraphim beside the throne have no trouble serving God because they've nothing in them to pull them away from it. They were made to serve God, and when they're engaged in that which comes naturally to them, they're like ducks when they go to the water, doing the thing natural to them, or bears in the wintertime curled up in their dens, following their nature. If you and I were what we should be, unfallen and without the stain of sin, we would be able to serve God without any effort. It would come natural and flow out like a fountain from the pressure beneath. But, sad to say, we're fallen.

34

Whenever God's people are down on their knees and pray, "Our Father in heaven, hallowed be Your name" (Matthew 6:9), they are doing the most natural thing in the world—not by their fallen nature, but because they were made in the image of God. When people turn their faces toward God, they are doing what He did in Adam and Eve during the time of innocence in the Garden of Eden—which is what we should be doing now. But because of the fall, we have been robbed of the power and desire to do this naturally. Sin remade our nature, thus it's not natural when we go to pray. We must override all the accumulated ages of sin if we are to say with sincerity, "Our Father in heaven." If sin hadn't entered the picture, we wouldn't have anything to override. Rather, we'd simply raise our voices like the songbirds that sing God's praises without effort.

People, then, tend to turn away from God, their desire and passion for Him growing cold, and go back to what comes natural to them. They change their minds or at least change their hearts. For it always begins with the heart. Many blame their circumstances and say, "It's my home life," or "My job keeps me so busy." "I've been buried in schoolwork." "I haven't been feeling well." "There's just not enough time in the day." Note how all of these are external things.

Again, backsliding begins in the heart. The backslider in heart will be filled with their own ways. God knows when our hearts are cooling off better and before we do. Then the individual figures it out, then one's church figures it out, and finally the world figures it out. That's typically the way it unfolds when someone backslides and goes back on their faith.

What does it mean to be a backslider in heart? To begin with, this person is one who is losing interest in the things of

God. They gradually revert back to the old ways, or perhaps they find some new and more refined sins than the ones they used to practice. The point, however, is that their hearts are cooling off toward God. The fire within is dwindling; it's not nearly what it was a few weeks or months or years prior. Slowly, love of God and communion with Him have turned distant and cold.

If you don't care to pray as much as you used to, then the only kind and honest thing I can say is that you're probably a backslider in heart. Because if you love God today as much as you loved Him before, wouldn't you want to pray now as much as you did before?

If a doctor runs a series of tests that shows a man's health is poor, what should the doctor do? Pat him on the shoulder and say, "Everything will be all right. Keep your chin up." No, that would prove the doctor to be incompetent, a disgrace to his profession. There is only one thing for the honest doctor to do, and that is to explain to the man the findings of the tests, and if the findings say he's not physically well, the doctor ought to tell him so, then offer the man expert advice, treatment, or medicine.

If you do not care to pray as much as you once did, ask yourself why and what might you do about it. Why has your heart cooled toward spending time with God? Perhaps communing with Him is not as sweet because other activities have crowded out the desire to pray. Modern life with its many distractions such as radio, television, newspapers, magazines, and automobiles that take us all over the countryside have a tendency to pull us away from our first love. But it starts in the heart, and again, these things are only external. They're not the causes. The cause lies deeper than that.

When someone is backslidden in heart, they often get bored being around earnest Christians. So if a glowing, earnest Christian bores you, if while in a group drinking coffee somebody brings up God or the Bible and this bothers you or embarrasses you, you'd best look to your own heart. Look seriously, because whenever talk of the Lord bores us, we may be sure there's something wrong inside.

I'm not referring here to those who introduce religion into impossible situations and do so out of habit without sincerity, without spontaneity, but only because they've been trained to do it, like a trained seal. Such people would bore anybody. But if an honest, glad-hearted Christian talks about God or spiritual things and it bores or embarrasses you, something has gone awry in your heart. The thing to do is to admit the truth, acknowledging it before God and seeking the Holy Spirit's counsel on the matter.

Be assured, the devil knows how to manipulate a Christian's backslidden condition to his own wicked advantage. Pray therefore that God will give you the strength and the understanding to avoid being manipulated by the enemy.

Heavenly Father, I pray You will enable me to recognize any backslidden aspect of my Christian life. I ask that You would give me the strength to address it and repent and have the Holy Spirit renew my spirit within. May my heart burn with longing for the spiritual disciplines that are before me. I pray this in Jesus' name, amen.

BACKSLIDING SOULS, RETURN TO GOD

Backsliding souls, return to God;
Your faithful God is gracious still;

37

Leave the false ways ye long have trod,
For God will your backslidings heal.

Your first espousals call to mind;
'Tis time ye should be now reclaimed.
What fruit could ever Christians find
In things whereof they're now ashamed?

The indignation of the Lord
Awhile endure, for 'tis your due;
But firm and steadfast stands his word;
Though you are faithless, he is true.

The blood of Christ, a precious blood!
Cleanses from all sin, doubt it not,
And reconciles the soul to God,
From every folly, every fault.

Joseph Hart (1759)

—4—

Symptoms
of Backsliding
the Devil Uses

The backslider in heart will be filled with his own ways, but a good man will be satisfied from above.

Proverbs 14:14

One symptom of backsliding in the heart is when someone develops a critical spirit toward others, especially toward preachers. Sometimes preachers are just plain, good, honest men who stand up and, sometimes with poor delivery and a few blunders, tell us in their simple way about God and what it means to be a Christian. People shrug and say, "He's all right," and only come to church in small numbers but with no zeal or enthusiasm.

We could well afford to humble ourselves and listen to anybody who has something to say about God, so long as the person is sincere with a heart to please the Lord. We should ask God to give us this same heart, a heart so sensitive that we are willing to receive instruction from anyone—except, that is, the hypocrites and pretenders, the exploiters, and those out to promote themselves instead of God.

When Charles Spurgeon was young, he attended a Methodist church service one stormy night. He slipped into the building and took a seat in the balcony only because he wanted to get out of the heavy rain. Someone in the congregation, who was no preacher at all, rose and exhorted everyone there to look straight to Jesus and be converted. Spurgeon later said, "I went in there a sinner, and when I came out, converted." He was converted by hearing a man who had no reputation, a layman who was leading a small prayer meeting.

We ought to be careful about judging others, be aware of our tendency to criticize unkindly. If it's a question of trying to improve, of raising the standards in writing and preaching, working to push ourselves and others to do things better, that's another matter and is perfectly all right. But if it is just criticism and sour feelings, do not allow the devil to use such attitudes, his purpose being to divide God's people and the Church.

Those who are critical of mediocre preaching are often in church only to keep up appearances. They aren't necessarily hypocritical since it's not a deliberate effort to deceive. But it's unfortunate that they aren't there because their hearts are warm and receptive. Shame or duty or fear or habit or custom or social pressure or something else has brought them. Many a pastor has cried, "Oh, God, what have I done or haven't done that my people are in such a condition?"

Solomon said, "The backslider in heart will be filled with his own ways, but a good man will be satisfied from above" (Proverbs 14:14).

So many people earn a reputation for being good Christians in churches and then secretly break fellowship with God. There is a lack of communion there, the fires of their souls burn low to the point they're hardly able anymore to feel any sense of God at all, and yet they've got a reputation they have to keep up. They may even allow themselves to get elected to boards, to lead young people's groups, prayer groups, choirs, and all the rest. But still the whole thing rings hollow because their hearts have slipped away.

Say you're a woman who has been married for ten years. If you positively knew that deep in his heart, your husband had no care for you at all, that deep in his heart lurked secret wishes that he's been fighting down, wishes that he might be rid of you and free from the necessity of being with you, how would you feel? That's backsliding in heart.

We want the love of people's hearts. We don't care so much about external things. If we want love, it's the love of the heart. How do you think God feels when He finds our hearts are slipping and we won't admit it to ourselves, even in our secret moments? How does He feel when we've gotten to a place where, if we told the truth, we'd have to admit we're bored with God and tired of being a Christian. We wouldn't say this out loud, we wouldn't admit it, but it's there all the same. Now, what do you imagine God thinks about that?

Jesus, in the book of Revelation, said, "Nevertheless I have this against you, that you have left your first love" (Revelation 2:4). He rebuked that church because He found what was happening way back there in the second century. He admonished that church because they were losing their affection for Him. There wasn't an Ephesian church elder, a preacher, a deacon, or any church member who dared to stand up and say, "I'm tired of God." Yet the heart of Jesus longed for affection, and it wasn't there. In essence, He's saying, "I don't feel the warmth I used to feel from you. Your smile is not as spontaneous. Your breath is not as sweet. The tone of your voice is not as kind as it once was. You have left your first love."

For a while, the backslider will keep up religious appearances with a hollow testimony and talk with enthusiastic Christians about God and seem to enjoy it. Paul Rader once said that this is akin to someone halfheartedly laughing at a joke when they hadn't gotten the point. How many hypocritical chuckles have I given in response to a joke I didn't think was funny? Rader was bold enough to apply that analogy to spiritual things. But over time it becomes difficult for such people to continue with the charade, to talk about the things of God, prayer, the Bible, and spiritual matters when their hearts aren't in it.

Unless we tire of this act, I'm afraid there's not much help. There are many who regularly attend church even though in their souls they're bored with the whole business. Maybe they heard somebody say, "Don't send your children to church, take them." And being steadfastly determined to follow this advice, they take their children to church. That's good, and I'm glad they do. It would be so much better, however, if their hearts were in it, so much better if going to church was more than a duty. So, for churchgoing Christians who in their hearts would rather turn their heads and go back to sleep, could this be evidence of leaving their first love?

In the matter of giving our tithes and offerings, warm-hearted people give spontaneously and love to do it. They give with joy because they want to give. Of course, giving can also be for show, whether I write a big check for missions or to help the poor. What kind of people would we be if we brought our offerings to God, knowing that by doing so, we will be more prosperous than if we didn't bring them; knowing that if we tithe, we'll have more than if we didn't tithe? When you take a ten-dollar bill from your wallet or purse and place it in the offering plate, you know you're out ten dollars, but you also know that God takes that ten and transmutes it into an everlasting blessing for humanity and puts into your heart a sense of joy. But giving out of habit when you have lost the joy of it is pretty tough. The backslider in heart will get enough of that after a while.

Paul said in Galatians 6:1, "Brethren, if a man is overtaken in any trespass, you who are spiritual restore such a one in a spirit of gentleness, considering yourself lest you also be tempted." One commentator points out that the words used here are medical terms, meaning when an arm or a shoulder gets out of joint.

Have you ever had a shoulder snap out of joint? One of my boys was hurt in football and had to sleep in a brace for a long time. It took a few years to get the strength back in that arm so it wouldn't snap out again. The Holy Spirit likened backsliding to a knee being out of joint. For someone to remain cheerful and keep smiling as though nothing were going on with their knee out of joint takes more heroic ability than I have. I pray that God will do us the inestimable favor of going from heart to heart, from soul to soul, and if there's a cooling off in there, to find it and cure it.

Shortly after the Lord Jesus was arrested, a woman spotted Peter in the crowd and asked him, "Are you one of His followers?" Peter responded, "No." She said, "I think you are. I know your accent." But Peter insisted, "I am not." She said again, "You are—your speech betrays you." Then he told her, "To prove I'm not a Christian, I'm going to do something no Christian would do." So he cursed, saying to himself, *If I don't curse and prove I'm not one of His followers, I may get arrested along with Jesus.*

At one point, Jesus turned back and looked into the eyes of the cursing apostle. Peter gazed into the face of Jesus, and what he saw there—hurt, pain, sorrow, longing, hope, and most of all, love—was too much for him. Running away from there, Peter stood outside and, with his face in his hands, sobbed bitterly. The Greek translation of the text indicates an uncontrolled torrent of weeping.

Jesus didn't say a word. Instead, He just looked at Peter.

"Be sober, be vigilant; because your adversary the devil walks about like a roaring lion, seeking whom he may devour. Resist him, steadfast in the faith . . ." (1 Peter 5:8–9). Though the temptations can be strong, and the flesh is certainly weak, let us not allow our hearts to cool toward the Lord.

Please, Lord Jesus, look at us in our hearts before it's too late. Don't let our hearts harden into permanent backsliding. We're no stronger than Peter. Look on us and make us weep, giving us the grace of tears this day so we do not leave our first love. In Jesus' name we pray, amen.

THE BACKSLIDER

Sad and lonely, weak and weary,
Down life's rugged path I roam;

Heart is bleeding, soul is weeping,
Seeking rest and finding none;
Father, once I dearly loved Thee,
In the happy days of yore,
But of love this world has robbed me,
Shall I never love Thee more?

O backslider, there is pardon,
Christ will save you from your sin,
Fill your yearning heart with gladness,
And receive you back again;
Come, oh, come, then, to the Savior,
Cast your doubts and fears away,
Plunge into the healing fountain,
There to save your soul today.

Here's a withered flow'r and faded,
Emblem of my lonely heart,
Once so full of love and duty,
Now lies crushed by human art;
Father, once my prayers were answered,
In the happy days of yore,
When in faith and love I sought Thee,
Wilt Thou never hear me more?

Life's a burden, Lord, without Thee,
Peace I nevermore can know,
All this world a sea of trouble,
All a wilderness of woe;
Father, leaving all, I seek Thee,
Plead once more to be forgiv'n;
Wash away my sins and sorrows,
Father, give me hope of heav'n.

Charles E. Orr (1900)

—5—

SELF-CONFIDENCE VS.
CONFIDENCE IN GOD

*My people are bent on backsliding from Me. Though they
call to the Most High, none at all exalt Him.*

Hosea 11:7

At the time this was written, Israel was in a state of what
the Scriptures call "backsliding." Hosea, two hundred years
prior, accused Israel of this backsliding: "Israel slideth back
as a backsliding heifer" (Hosea 4:16 KJV). The old prophets
were not as genteel as many preachers are now, but they
were a great deal more effective. They weren't just smooth—
they got their ideas across with power. Hosea knew he was
talking to people who were more or less country people,
farm people, cattle raisers, and shepherds. The young heifer
was led forward, and for no apparent reason, she suddenly

decided she'd had enough and refused to go another inch. The more they pulled her, the more she backed up. Later, Hosea said, "My people are bent on backsliding from Me."

Through Jeremiah, God told them at length of His moral displeasure and the necessity for judgment. I say necessity for judgment because judgment for sin is sure; it is not the result of vengeful anger on God's part. It lies in the moral structure of the world. A moral God created a moral universe, and the breaking of moral laws results in chaos and destruction. The judgment God spoke of relates to sin as cause does to effect or effect to cause. If someone swallows a capsule of cyanide, it isn't the vengeance of God or His anger that causes death to follow instantly. God may look with a pitying eye upon it, but the person perishes swiftly nevertheless because it lies within cyanide to be destructive of the human organism. Sin is like that. The man of God said that the people were bent on backsliding, but then he added, "If you will return, then I will bring you again."

But what is this backsliding business? I've talked about it in previous chapters, but there is still more to cover. Adam and Eve were the first, and down through the years, judgment followed sin, or they returned to God and were forgiven.

As mentioned earlier, those Christians who backslide tend to have less taste for praying than they used to have. We pray with less joy and engage in prayer less frequently.

We are backsliding when we have lost the relish for the Bible we once had. When first converted, the Bible was a wonderful book to us; we opened the Word of God with great joy and read it day and night. So if we no longer relish the Bible, we are most assuredly falling into spiritual decline.

We are backsliding when we're more tolerant of evil than we once were, when we don't have that horror of sin that we pray and sing about. Almost every newly converted Christian has that horror, but little by little we get more and more tolerant, and in this way the devil can gain a foothold, leading us astray. Now, there's a place for tolerance, but there's also a place for intolerance. When it comes to evil, there's only one attitude for the Christian, and that is intolerance. So if we are less intolerant of sin that we used to recoil from, if we hate sin less than we used to hate it, we are backsliding.

We are backsliding when we have less enthusiasm for spiritual things than we used to have. If we find we have less enthusiasm than we had two weeks ago, two months ago, or two years ago, the honest thing to do is to admit we've cooled off and are in a backslide.

We are backsliding when we take greater liberties with our conscience than we used to take. The conscience is a beautiful thing. The Holy Spirit is on the side of conscience, our inward mentor, instructor, and moral guide who warns us of approaching danger. The conscience is like a radar within our spirits that tells us when the enemy plane has taken off to destroy us. It is a sensitivity of the heart. So when we become less sensitive and take greater liberties with our consciences, as if to say "I'm broader now," that's a sign of backsliding.

We are backsliding when our sympathies begin to wither away, when they aren't as strong as they used to be, and when we give of our time or money with less pleasure. There was a time when we gave with a good deal of pleasure. We put our offering in for the poor, for missions or some worthy cause, or for the church, and we gave it with joy. We thanked the

Lord for the privilege of giving. We may still give, but it's without joy now, without relish.

Of course, God doesn't need our offerings, yet He looks on us with pleasure when we give with a heart of gratitude. He loves cheerfulness in giving, and He doesn't love any other kind. There was a time in our early Christian life when we may have given a large amount to the Lord, but then business got heavier and we had investments, and we had to borrow, and we had more children, and they grew up and had to go to college, and so now we give less and we excuse it. That's backsliding; we might as well admit it, not try to hide behind the trees of the garden from the voice of the Lord.

We are backsliding when we boast more than we used to, when we act as though we can do things just fine on our own, in our own strength. Whenever we indulge our impulse to boast or become careless of speech, that is evidence and another symptom. The purest and humblest speech in the world should be the speech of the Christian.

Hosea, who wrote long before Jeremiah, gave us one of the greatest chapters in the Bible, the fourteenth chapter, the last of his book, where he wrote, "O Israel, return to the LORD your God" (v. 1). He didn't say return to the church, although of course that's an important thing to do. But rather he said "return to the LORD your God." David said, "Against You, You only, have I sinned" (Psalm 51:4). So if you've sinned against everybody on your block, everybody in your part of the city, remember that finally you've sinned against God only. Return to the Lord your God, for you have fallen by your iniquity, and there isn't any other way to fall.

Some people say their business or job has dragged them down. No, you fell because of your iniquity. Somebody else says my wife is not sympathetic. You get right, and stay right, and don't blame your husband or your wife. Remember, God said, "My people are prone to backsliding," but here the Lord says, "I will heal their backsliding. I will immunize them against it. I will take away that proneness."

I don't think there will ever be a time when the humble Christian can stop singing, "Prone to wander, Lord, I feel it. Prone to leave the God I love." These words come from Robert Robinson's hymn "Come, Thou Fount of Every Blessing." We're telling the truth when we say, "Prone to wander, Lord, I feel it." If you don't think you are prone to wander, try not praying for a few weeks. Stop reading your Bible for a while, or stop fellowshipping with God's people. It won't be long and you will start to wander.

Jesus Christ says, "I'll heal your backsliding by getting at the wheel myself." And so long as He's there, you won't backslide.

It's difficult for us to believe that the Lord loves us as much when we're backsliding as He does when we're not, but it's true nevertheless. It's there in the Bible: "I will heal their backsliding, I will love them freely, for My anger has turned away from him. I will be like the dew to Israel; he shall grow like the lily, and lengthen his roots like Lebanon. His branches shall spread; his beauty shall be like an olive tree, and his fragrance like Lebanon" (Hosea 14:4–6).

Do you remember the people who used to dwell under your shadow, those who looked up to you, who came to you for prayer and help? They had allowed their lives to deteriorate; those who dwelt under your shadow have all gone away from you. You're no help anymore to them. But God reverses all that, saying, "Those who dwell under his shadow shall return . . ." (Hosea 14:7). It's as if he were talking to a tree that once had full lush leaves growing in greenness, with cattle lying down underneath it. The sheep would crowd in, and the birds would fly in out of the summer heat and build their nests there. Then something happened to the tree, and the leaves all fell off, never coming back. It was no good for shade anymore, no good for building a nest there anymore, and so the cattle and the birds fled. The tree was no good to any of its fellow creatures. Then God touched the tree, and it burst again into bloom and leaf, and the cows and sheep and birds all returned to the tree.

God said "return," and that's what Jacob did at Bethel. That's what the prodigal son did when he said, "I will return again and go back to my father." That's what every backslider must do. I have a version of the Old Testament that was translated out of Hebrew into Greek years before the birth of Christ by seventy Hebrew scholars, and for that reason it is called the Septuagint. Then George Washington's secretary, a learned man and a great Greek scholar, took this Greek Septuagint, which had been translated from the Hebrew, and brought it over into English. I like the way he translated Jeremiah 15:19, where God says, "Therefore thus saith the LORD, if thou will return, I will reinstate thee, and in my presence, thou shall stand." Now, the King James version isn't much different: "If thou return, then will I bring thee again, and thou shalt stand before me." But *reinstatement*—that is exactly what our poor hearts cry out for. We want to be reinstated in the grace and in the sense of His presence: ". . . and in my presence, thou shall stand."

If you took a frightened baby from the poorest home in the country to the richest, where there's luxurious furnishings and silk bedsheets, the child would still cry its little eyes out and never be satisfied until its mother came. You could say, "Honey, don't you realize this mansion you're in cost a million dollars? The furniture was imported from Italy and Germany. The rugs come from Turkey, the silk from Japan. Your dinner table is filled with pure Wedgwood china." You'd still hear the baby howl because nothing will bring peace to the heart of that little one but its mother.

If the mother walked in and embraced the child, that would be all that was necessary. In the same way, God says, "I will reinstate thee, and in my presence, thou shall stand." You can't continue to backslide and not lose the presence and fellowship of God. You will be a miserable person filled with the misery of your own ways.

John Wesley wrote, "Yes, from this instant now, I will to my offended Father cry; my base ingratitude I feel, vilest of all thy children, I; not worthy to be called thy son; yet will I thee, my Father, own." That's the prayer and the song of a man who feels he isn't where he used to be. "O God," Wesley prayed, "I used to love to pray, and I don't love to pray. I used to love the Bible, but now it's pretty tasteless. I used to have a fine conscience that kept me right and carefree. I used to like the fellowship of the saints, but it's not so anymore. I'm not worthy of being called thy son, yet I will call thee Father."

When the Lord took you in, blessed you, and held you close in His arms, He knew that you were a transgressor. You may say to yourself, "I've disappointed God," but how could you disappoint somebody who knew what you did before you did it and knew the end from the beginning? You only disappoint somebody when they don't know you and they think you're better than you are. But God doesn't think you're better than you are; He knows.

Now, I warn you that if you're a true child of God and persist in a lukewarm state, God promises to chasten you. "Behold, I have refined you, but not as silver; I have tested you in the furnace of affliction" (Isaiah 48:10). If a back-slidden child of God refuses to repent and will not admit they have cooled off, having lost their first love, they will then face God's chastening judgment. I do not mean harsh punishment or destruction, but rather discipline, to bring into order again. "For whom the LORD loves He chastens" (Hebrews 12:6).

Paul said, "Therefore whoever eats this bread or drinks this cup of the Lord in an unworthy manner will be guilty of the body and blood of the Lord. But let a man examine himself, and so let him eat of the bread and drink of the cup. For he who eats and drinks in an unworthy manner eats and drinks judgment to himself, not discerning the Lord's body. For this reason many are weak and sick among you, and many sleep. For if we would judge ourselves, we would not be judged. But when we are judged, we are chastened by the Lord, that we may not be condemned with the world" (1 Corinthians 11:27–32).

I fear the chastening hand of God because His chastening hand is sometimes heavy. He knows you're too valuable to treat lightly. If it's a burnt potato or some cheap trifle that can be bought at the market for a few pennies, it may be thrown out. But if it's silver or gold, it must be refined, for it's too precious to lose. He says, "I have refined you, but not the way silver is refined. I have purified you, but not the way gold is purified. I have purified you in the furnace of affliction." Sometimes our very afflictions are the chastening of God that we might not be condemned to the world. But then He says to us, "If you return, I'll reinstate you, and you shall dwell in My presence." And God could offer us nothing greater in all the wide world than that.

I praise Thee, heavenly Father, for the graciousness of Your forgiveness. I have fallen so many times, but Your grace has always brought me back to where You want me to be. Thy grace is infinitely bigger than my sin. In Jesus' name I pray, amen.

ARISE, MY SOUL, ARISE

Arise, my soul, arise;
shake off thy guilty fears;
the bleeding Sacrifice
in my behalf appears.
Before the throne my Surety stands;
my name is written on his hands.

He ever lives above,
for me to intercede,
his all-redeeming love,
his precious blood to plead.
His blood atoned for ev'ry race,
and sprinkles now the throne of grace.

Five bleeding wounds he bears,
received on Calvary;
they pour effectual prayers;
they strongly plead for me.

"Forgive him, O forgive," they cry,
"nor let that ransomed sinner die!"

My God is reconciled;
his pard'ning voice I hear.
He owns me for his child,
I can no longer fear.
With confidence I now draw nigh,
and "Father, Abba, Father!" cry.

Charles Wesley (1742)

—6—

How We Can Prevent the Devil from Taking Advantage of Us

But I determined this within myself, that I would not come again to you in sorrow. For if I make you sorrowful, then who is he who makes me glad but the one who is made sorrowful by me? And I wrote this very thing to you, lest, when I came, I should have sorrow over those from whom I ought to have joy, having confidence in you all that my joy is the joy of you all.

2 Corinthians 2:1–3

Contrary to what many Christians think, life is not a game but warfare. Everything depends on what approach we take to the Christian life. If we imagine the Christian life to be a game, we'll treat it that way. When the Western team plays the Eastern team, or when the Yankees play the Dodgers, it is but a game. There may be a little money in it and a little glory, but it's a game, and nobody gets killed. When it comes to warfare, however, when a soldier marches out onto the battlefield, he doesn't go out to win a game. He goes out to kill or be killed, to live or to die. And in a spiritual sense, as well as a real sense, this is true of the Christian life.

We're at war, and this is not a cold war but a hot war, and one with the cruelest and most deadly enemy ever known. And that enemy does not consist of the helmeted soldiers of a human emperor, president, or prime minister. No soldier or enemy anywhere could be as cruel, as utterly sadistic and evil as the antagonist we fight. I'm speaking, of course, of the devil. He hates God. In fact, he hates anything good, anything that has God's name stamped on it. He hates all the souls on earth, especially those escaping from his clutches, and therefore he wages war in an all-out effort to ruin every human being.

All Christians must keep this mindset: We face an enemy who is fighting to ruin us completely. He means to tear us apart, destroy our Christian testimony and unity, and sabotage all the churches and families he can in the time he has left. That's his business.

In this war, there are no rules on the devil's part. He honors no Geneva Convention or anything like that. He has an advantage over us because he has no rules and attacks at will. The gang member or burglar has an advantage over the decent citizen because the decent citizen recognizes ethical, moral, and legal restrictions, while the outlaw recognizes none. So Satan has this advantage as he roams about in the fallen world, looking for those he can ambush, no matter who they are—young or old, rich or poor, innocent or guilty. He's out to deceive, disrupt, and destroy.

So how can we keep the devil from gaining the upper hand in our lives? Here are some ways the enemy will try:

First, he's given an advantage whenever we tolerate wrongdoing. Of course, tolerance is a virtue when it comes to having patience toward those with views or opinions divergent from one's own, yet we still live and work beside them in what is called peaceful coexistence. Tolerance is a virtue when it means showing patience with those who have tastes different from ours, for we cannot all be alike. Even Christians can't all be alike. We must recognize this and allow people a certain latitude for their humanity's sake. So tolerance is a virtue; it means living at peace with other races, cultures, languages, and religions.

But there is another kind of tolerance, which is to tolerate that which God abominates. If you allow that into your home, business, or life anywhere, Satan will get an advantage. What God abominates is not a virtue, and regardless of how much trouble it gets you in or how much persecution, what God abominates should not be tolerated by the Christian.

Consider Eli in the Old Testament. Eli was a priest who had two sons, Hophni and Phinehas. Eli tolerated wickedness in these young men. When they grew old enough to become priests, Eli was too weak to say no. So he permitted his sons to get away with murder. The result was that the Ark of God was taken, Hophni and Phinehas were both slain, the wife of one of them died in childbirth, Eli fell and broke his neck, and the priesthood passed from him to Samuel's line. "Now the sons of Eli were corrupt; they did not know the LORD" (1 Samuel 2:12).

You can't help what your children do when they're not at home, but you can help what they do when they are at home. That is what happened to a man who tolerated what God abominated. Some say that I am a bit hard and want to know why I do certain things. I want to be as gentle as possible with people but not allow them to allow into the Church that which is evil. So keep evil out; keep it as far out as you can. Enough of it will get in that you don't know about without allowing any of it to enter that you do know about.

The Israelites tolerated sin among them, and the result was that they alienated themselves from God and invited desolation upon Israel. For many years they were in trouble with the Midianites, the Canaanites, the Philistines, and all the rest because God withdrew His protection and because they tolerated what God abominated. If we tolerate behavior, habits, and attitudes that are wrong and sinful, we will give the devil an advantage in our lives. It's like going into the boxing ring with one hand tied behind your back. You've got enough of an enemy on your hands without deliberately putting yourself at a disadvantage.

But on the flip side, another way we give the devil an advantage is by being too severe with wrongdoers. The apostle Paul once prayed, hoping for a man to repent before his body was destroyed. And as soon as Paul found out that he'd repented, he said, "Now whom you forgive anything, I also forgive. For if indeed I have forgiven anything, I have forgiven that one for your sakes in the presence of Christ, lest Satan should take advantage of us; for we are not ignorant of his devices" (2 Corinthians 2:10–11).

Every church ought to have that rule; every mother and father ought to have that rule. Don't tolerate wickedness in your children, but don't bring up their pasts to them again if they repent and try to do better.

Paul felt the transgressor had already been punished enough by the displeasure of the Corinthian crowd and by his own conscience. When God, to punish Israel, allowed a certain king to come against Israel, He then turned on that king and said, "I was punishing My people, and you are adding to the punishment." So He punished the people who had punished Israel with too great a harshness toward the weak and the poor. In other words, God allowed Israel to be punished, but He didn't put up with the punishers going overboard.

"There go I but by the grace of God," said John Wesley when he saw a man stagger down the street. Nobody has any right to look down their religious nose at anybody, regardless of who they are.

To strike a balance between tolerating the wrong or not tolerating the wrong and yet being patient with the wrongdoer takes more grace and wisdom than you and I have. God has to help us with this; if He doesn't, we give the devil an advantage. Where we're too hard on people, the devil grabs that and runs with it. And where we're too easy on sin, the devil grabs that and runs with it. So let's watch out that we don't play into his hands in either case.

———

Another way we can allow the devil to get an advantage is when we're cast down by defeat. You say, "Aren't you a preacher known to have what people call the deeper life, the victorious life?" Yes, but I'm a realist too. I don't believe in saying "I'm feeling fine" when I'm sick or pale and can hardly stand. There isn't any reason to claim the sun is shining today in Chicago when there's a steady drizzle coming down. There's no virtue in being unrealistic. John Wesley said, "You'll never hinder the cause of Christ by admitting your sin, but you will hinder it if you cover your sin."

Defeat does come to people. People are sometimes defeated in their lives, hopes, plans, and labors. I've never been very successful, but I've never been a complete failure either. I am wondering how I'd take it if the church board were to call me in and say, "You've been around long enough; it's been nice knowing you."

Or if the New York office were to call me and say, "You've been editor long enough. Would you kindly send us your typewriter?" I don't know how I'd take it. So I'm giving you something here I don't know too much about myself, which is how I would handle the total failure of plans and labors, failure in personal living, and what it means to fall flat on your face and then have the grace of God lift you out of it.

Still, we will give the devil an advantage if we get cast down by defeat. There's nothing terrible about falling, but you will have trouble if you give up and stay lying down. Falling is final only when we accept it as final. Those who raise a hand and cry "Lord, please help me" will receive the strength needed to get back on their feet again.

Maybe you made a New Year's resolution and within a week you broke it, and that's par for the course for you. Brethren, don't get cast down. Some of God's dear people are always dragging their feet. They're never quite able to rise and face life's challenges. If that's you, ask God to cleanse and heal you. Don't wait and let things fester. If you cut your finger but don't do anything about it, it could become infected. But if you deal with it immediately, you can catch it quickly and begin healing.

Likewise, God offers first aid to His people. It's there in 1 John 1:8–9 and in 2:1–2, where John wrote, "If we say that we have no sin, we deceive ourselves, and the truth is not in us. If we confess our sins, He is faithful and just to forgive us our sins and to cleanse us from all unrighteousness." There is no reason for anybody to walk around with a stain on their soul, because God has provided a remedy. The blood of Jesus Christ is "the propitiation for our sins, and not for ours only but also for the whole world" (1 John 2:2). So remember that if your soul has suffered defeat or your plans have been dashed and you feel paralyzed, if you allow such things to discourage you and cast you down, you will play straight into the hands of the devil.

Another way we can play into the devil's hands is when we are elated by victory. I once knew a preacher who would say such things as, "Oh, we had a wonderful meeting with a fine atmosphere." He was a religious meteorologist and always had to have the right atmosphere before feeling good about it. There is such a thing as being victorious and *not* having a very pleasant atmosphere in which to be victorious. The portion, however, for every Christian is peace and joy and a certain delight in worshiping a perfect, unchanging God.

Here is the Christian's philosophy: If we have God, even if we experience a victory, we can't have anything more than God. And even if we suffer a defeat, we can't have anything less than God. Either way, we always have God. If the children of the Lord would only remember that when they have God, they have everything in one package. When God has you, and you have Him, there is no such thing as permanent defeat. If you are defeated, you don't lose anything, and if you're victorious, you don't gain anything, because you have God, win or lose.

It will take your lifetime and perhaps several thousand years in the world to develop this attitude, and perhaps, God being infinite, it will take an eternity to develop it all. No success can elate me, and no defeat can beat me down, but I still have God.

The good preachers, if they are any good at all, admit that they haven't learned much. Nonetheless, they study three books. They study first the Bible. Then they study their own hearts, and finally they study other people. And in those three books, they get all they need—the Word of the Living God, themselves, and others. And the Word of God gives them a thousand keys, which can be used to unlock a thousand secrets in their own hearts and in the hearts of other people.

And in my study of people, I've found that some were born under a gloomy cloud or maybe they shot an albatross at some point because everything they do turns into defeat for them. On the other hand, after a sermon is preached or a hymn sung, some people come to you with tears in their eyes and express how their hearts were blessed. That person is in a spiritual attitude that can get help. I once preached a very ordinary sermon, and a man approached me afterward with a big smile and said, "My heart hasn't been warmed so much in years as when I heard that sermon." Well, it wasn't that great of a sermon really; it was just some truth given. But here was a man whose heart was in a spiritual condition ready to receive the truth.

Having a gloomy attitude can also play into the hands of the devil, giving him an advantage. And being a fault-finder can lead to such gloominess. Another time, a person came to me and said, "I was getting defeated in my heart, and things weren't going so well until one day I discovered what it was: I had been criticizing you." So we can be harsh critics and faultfinders and give the devil an advantage that way.

The beloved John was the sharpest critic the Church ever had, but it was kindly done, expressed with love and concern. We don't have to accept everything; we can be critical, gently pointing out shortcomings, and ask God for a remedy. All prophets and apostles down through the centuries have done that. But it's quite another thing to be a faultfinder.

Satan is a criminal, and every criminal establishes an unconscious pattern. Every law-enforcement expert, criminologist, and cop knows this if they have been on the job for any length of time. They learn that crime has a strange way of repeating itself. If a man is a burglar, he always burgles in the same way. It's very rare that he changes his modus operandi. The devil is the criminal of the universe, but he isn't quite wise enough to escape his pattern.

God says that if we will but read His Word and pray, "I'll teach you the patterns so you'll never need to fall into the devil's traps. You'll know the devil when you see him and smell him." We're not ignorant of his devices. In all of these tricks, there is a certain sameness, and we defeat the enemy when we can recognize what they are and then, by the grace of God, avoid them.

How can we know the devil's devices and tricks? By the light of the Word of God, by praying for wisdom, and by the Holy Spirit's illumination. Peter once played right into the devil's hands when Jesus said He was going to His death. Peter responded, "Not so." Jesus said to Peter, "Get behind Me, Satan! You are an offense to Me, for you are not mindful of the things of God, but the things of men" (Matthew 16:23). Jesus knew that this was the devil speaking through Peter, who had played into the hands of the devil, speaking not as from heaven, but from earth.

By God's grace, let us watch out for and stay clear of the enemy's traps. Nothing I can say will save you from stumbling unless you search the Scriptures for yourself, pray, and trust the Holy Spirit to illuminate your heart. Let's each of us endeavor to be obedient, loving, and trustful. The outcome will be a victorious life.

Heavenly Father, the battle is before me, and I need Your help and discernment to identify who my enemy really is. Give me the courage to stand against him, and let your Word strengthen and lead me in the right direction. I pray this in Jesus' name, amen.

O GOD, OUR HELP IN AGES PAST

O God, our help in ages past,
our hope for years to come,
our shelter from the stormy blast,
and our eternal home:

Under the shadow of your throne
your saints have dwelt secure;

sufficient is your arm alone,
and our defense is sure.

Before the hills in order stood,
or earth received its frame,
from everlasting you are God,
to endless years the same.

A thousand ages in your sight
are like an evening gone,
short as the watch that ends the night
before the rising sun.

Time, like an ever-rolling stream,
soon bears us all away;
we fly forgotten, as a dream
dies at the op'ning day.

O God, our help in ages past,
our hope for years to come,
still be our guard while troubles last,
and our eternal home!

                        Isaac Watts (1719)

—7—

How God Uses Trials and Disappointments

Thus says the Lord: "You shall not go up nor fight against your brethren the children of Israel. Let every man return to his house, for this thing is from Me." Therefore they obeyed the word of the Lord, and turned back, according to the word of the Lord.

1 Kings 12:24

Rehoboam was the son of Solomon, and he had become king following his father's death. He had listened to the bad advice of his counselors and took certain political actions, which alienated a part of the nation.

Jeroboam, an ambitious man, had taken part in the nation's leadership, declaring he wanted to become the king. Rehoboam wanted to try to stop this by going to war, but he had just enough ability to hear God still to hear Him say,

"You shall not go up nor fight against your brethren the children of Israel. Let every man return to his house, for this thing is from Me."

God told Solomon that his kingdom would be divided, and now Solomon was gone. Even so, God was carrying out His plan, which was taking place before the eyes of Solomon's son. His son was going to throw himself in to try to straighten things out, but God said, "Don't you do it."

That's the historical circumstance that gave us the beautiful Scripture verse at the start of this chapter. The words here are among the most liberating and consoling of the Bible. Yet the truth suggested is developed and strengthened throughout the Bible until, in the New Testament, it shines like the sun, bringing light, warmth, and health to us all. It is simply this: Whatever comes to a Christian and servant of the Lord is from God.

We know that natural laws govern the natural world, and these laws are administered impartially, so that "you may be sons of your Father in heaven; for He makes His sun rise on the evil and on the good, and sends rain on the just and on the unjust" (Matthew 5:45). Grain and the fruit of harvest come to believers and unbelievers alike. And sickness and pain visit not only bad people but also good people. There is loss, and there is sorrow. The loss and sorrow come as certainly and as frequently to the forgiven Christian as to those mired in their sin. Death, too, will visit both the children of God and the lost, "as it is appointed for men to die once" (Hebrews 9:27). All of this occurs according to the law of cause and effect that governs the natural world, which we are helpless to change. This thought has given us all the sad and beautiful poetry of the world.

The English poet Edward FitzGerald, in his translation of Omar Khayyam's poems, wrote, "We are no other than a moving row / Of Magic Shadow-shapes that come and go . . ." FitzGerald goes on to liken human beings to checkers: "'Tis all a Chequer-board of Nights and Days / Where Destiny with Men for pieces plays: / Hither and thither moves, and mates, and slays, / And one by one back in the closet lays." Others have compared the individual person to a football being kicked or a cork floating on the water.

While all of this is true, the poet fails to take Christ into consideration. There is a natural world filled with people, and natural laws govern this world. An observer might well conclude that humankind is simply a roll of magic shadow-shapes that come and go, or that each of us is a checker played on the checkerboard of life. And that is both accurate and realistic, not necessarily pessimistic, and yet it takes our Lord Jesus Christ out of the equation.

I have excellent news: Christians do not fall wholly under this law. Believers have entered a new kingdom, and in this kingdom all things are different. Christians may poetically describe themselves as if a football, but they smile wryly when they feel themselves being kicked because they know they're being kicked toward a certain goal. They may still feel as if they are a checker being played on a vast checkerboard, but in this new place in the kingdom of God, they also know they're not subject to the laws of chance.

They may feel that they are but dust, as the psalmist tells us in God's Word, but their trust in His promises confirms they're being blown gently toward home, heaven, and the Father. They may feel they are like a cork, bobbing up and down in depression and boom, sickness and health, loss and gain, sorrow and joy, and may feel themselves being carried away on the undulating waves of time, yet by faith they know positively that they're under the watchful eye of God. And the Father will guide them through this life until they are safely with Him.

Have you ever stopped to consider what our world would be like in twenty-four hours if God said, "I'm going to give everybody everything they want. All they have to do is wish for it, and they will get it." If we all lived in such a fairy tale as this, what a world we'd be living in.

Think about the weather, for instance. If it's baseball season, we want it warm; if it's football season, we want it cool. If the church is going to have a picnic, they want it dry; the people with lawns want rain. A farmer wants the calm, hot air to make the crops grow, while the city dweller with the fog and smog wants a wind to carry the fog and smog away. So you'd never find people agreeing on much. The old man wants it quiet, and the young fellow wants it noisy and full of life. We couldn't get together because we don't want the same things, and sometimes we don't even know what we want.

We don't know what we want because we don't know ourselves. We don't know the world around us very well. We don't know the future at all. And we don't know the past except sketchily, and we don't know what's good for us. If we all had our druthers with the world around us, it would be one of the worst things that could happen to us. It would be like three-year-olds having their druthers with meals. They would never eat anything good for them. Instead, they would fill up on sweets and suffer for the rest of the night. They would never become mature, healthy citizens. So we must impose discipline to help our children grow up, teaching them what's good for them.

That's exactly where we are in the kingdom of God. Even though we're Christians and born of the Spirit, we still don't always know what's good for us. So God must choose for us. "He will choose our inheritance for us, the excellence of Jacob whom He loves" (Psalm 47:4). He chooses and sends us the things we ought to have.

That doesn't preclude prayer, of course, as the Holy Spirit tells us what we ought to pray for, and thus we can help shape events through our Spirit-inspired prayers. But if you think of your life in the long sweep of circumstances between the time you were converted until your death, you will be glad that God will be choosing your inheritance for you. I could go to the Bible and show you about six different circumstances that have come to men and women, and we can write after every one of them, *This thing is from God.* He picks out our inheritance. And when we look at it and say, "I don't want that," God replies, "Son, Daughter, this thing is from me." And blessed is the Christian who knows how to accept it.

But how does temptation fit into this? Why, as Christians, are we being tempted? I like to answer in the language of the officer in response to the rookie soldier, who took off at a run when the enemy started shooting at him. The officer asked the young soldier, "What do you think you're out here for?" When a Christian comes and says, "Pastor, I'm being tempted," I want to reply, "Well, you're a soldier now. You're in a fight. And what do you think you're here for if it isn't to get shot at?"

When our Lord was tempted in the wilderness, He was tempted by a cruel enemy, and His temptations were real and valid. He was tempted for two reasons: to know that He might be perfected for His life's work, and to learn obedience through the things He suffered.

When Satan found that he couldn't get the Son of God to sin, the devil skulked away from Him. The Lord Jesus Christ was proof against the temptations of the devil, and He caused that same devil to lose face and caused hell to shudder to its foundations. How else could God have given a testimony of hell and earth to Jesus if it had not been through temptation?

When our Lord was forty days hungry and in great anguish of body as well as weariness of mind after having been tempted so bitterly, don't you think in His human heart He might have said, "Why must this happen to me?" The Father's answer was, "This thing is from me. I've allowed this experience to come to you. You're not alone. I've been with you, and you're being tempted in my will."

Now, that ought to encourage all of us. If you're being cruelly and bitterly tempted, don't let this get you down. Even amid the temptations, God says, "This thing is from me." So cease worrying and abusing yourself, lashing yourself like the Flagellants and saying, "I am no good. I will whip myself. I'm being tempted." Of course you're being tempted. The servant is not better than their Lord. This thing is from God.

But what about persecution? The passage at the end of Genesis shows us a wonderful thing. Joseph was sold into slavery in Egypt for a small amount of money and was thrown in jail, suffering through years of imprisonment. Later on, however, when his brethren came down, Joseph was second in power to the king himself, running all of Egypt as a prime minister. When Joseph made himself known to them, they wept, and Joseph said to them, "But as for you, you meant evil against me; but God meant it for good, in order to bring it about as it is this day, to save many people alive" (Genesis 50:20).

As poor Joseph was going through his persecution, there is no doubt he wondered why God had allowed it. His brethren were persecuting him, but God said, "Don't get excited. This thing is from me to persecute you and save many people's lives."

And what about failure? Peter denied his Lord, and we would have to admit, it was a failure. But long before Peter lied, used profane language, and denied his Lord, the Lord had foreseen this event. "And the Lord said, 'Simon, Simon! Indeed, Satan has asked for you, that he may sift you as wheat. But I have prayed for you, that your faith should not fail; and when you have returned to Me, strengthen your brethren'" (Luke 22:31–32).

The prayers of Jesus had been prevailing, and they were put to heaven effectually for Peter's sake before the disciple was tempted by this sin. Our Lord Jesus saw Peter as a half bushel of chaff and wheat, but Peter saw himself as just a bushel of wheat. He didn't see the chaff at all. The devil wanted to destroy Peter. So the Lord said, "All right, devil, go ahead and shake him and sift him and blow on him a while."

The devil no doubt smiled one of his devilish smiles and said, "I'm going to get at Peter." So he shook him and sifted him, and Peter, in the middle of it all, became morally dizzy and denied his Lord. Yet when the sifting was over, the chaff was all gone, and Peter was reduced to what he had been the whole time: a quart of wheat and fifty quarts of chaff. Peter thought he was all wheat, and the devil thought he was all chaff. But Jesus knew he was part chaff and part wheat, so He got rid of the chaff.

We all tend to overrate ourselves. We like to mull over our successes and what people think of us, and we are likely to get the notion that we're better than we are. When God tells us the truth, sometimes we don't want to believe it. Jesus said to Peter, "Peter, you will deny me." Peter replied, "Me, deny you? Oh no. These others may, but not I." But then he did what he swore he wouldn't do. And the Lord smiled and said, "This thing is from me, Peter." And after Peter had been loved back into fellowship with his Lord, he never made that mistake again. The Lord used Peter's failure.

Maybe you have failed recently. If so, there's no reason for you to keep saying to yourself, "I'm no good." No, you're not good. None of us are. Still, we have One who loves us despite our failures, so much so that He died for us to secure our salvation. And He made us the apple of His eye, and He wrote it in His hands, in His heart, and on His shoulders, so we must be worth something after all. When we fail Him, we must remember: "This thing is from me." Now, if we will bow our heads and ask Him to forgive us for failing Him, we'll recall how small and weak we are, how desperately we need the Lord, and how to trust Him better than we did.

There are also trials of bereavement. Consider the man Lazarus who died while Jesus traveled. Jesus came late to the scene, and when He arrived, Lazarus was already in the grave. Jesus went to the grave and said, "Lazarus come forth." And Lazarus came forth. But he didn't come forth alone. Do you know what came forth out of the grave with Lazarus? The eleventh chapter of John. Among other things, John gives us these precious words of Jesus: "I am the resurrection and the life. He who believes in Me, though he may die, he shall live" (11:25).

Since the day John recorded these words of Jesus, a light has been glowing in more graves than we could ever count. And this one verse has offered hope to countless people who have lost their loved ones and given comfort to millions of believers while on their deathbeds. Lazarus didn't walk out of that grave alone; the hopeful, brilliant, vibrant eleventh chapter of John came out with him. "This thing is from me. I let you die," said Jesus, "in order that this might be a ladder to the coming ages to climb on; this might be a victory over the grave. This might be a light for all those who believe."

There are trials and tribulations. I read recently about a ship at sea where, during a violent storm, the bow of the vessel became stuck on a sandbar, while the stern was getting thrashed by the wind and the waves. The ship broke apart into pieces, and everybody leaped out, grabbed a board from the ruined ship, and swam safely to shore.

The apostle Paul had his share of tribulations. He said that for fourteen days and fourteen nights, they hadn't seen the sun or a single star, and they were without adequate food in their little old-fashioned ship, being tossed in the terror of the Mediterranean Sea.

But God said, "Don't worry, Paul, this thing is from me." And what was the result? The light of Christianity reached pagan Rome, and many lives were saved. To Paul, the situation may have looked as if somebody was picking on him, but to God, it was all part of a greater purpose.

Another example from the Bible is the story of a man who was born blind, and his parents grieved terribly over it. Their little boy couldn't see, and later when he began to stumble and fall and run into things and hurt himself, no doubt bitterness seeped into his parents' hearts. Or if there wasn't bitterness, perhaps there was puzzlement as they asked themselves, "Why was our child born blind?"

But that same man born blind found Jesus Christ because of his condition. If he'd been a seeing man, he might well have been out working instead of sitting by the wayside. But because he was not a seeing man, he was shut up in the dark precincts of his mind. His ears were sharp, however, and he heard the sound of the passing footsteps. Who was it? It was Jesus of Nazareth. The man cried, "Son of David, have mercy on me." He found the Lord, rose, and followed Him, and is now with the Father in heaven for eternity. "This thing is from me."

There are smaller disappointments that come our way. All we want is our way. Picture a twelve-year-old boy who, on the Saturday morning of a planned picnic, jumps out of bed and looks out the window and sees rain pouring down. That is the agony and sharp bite of disappointment. The good time he was going to have that day is ruined. Disappointment and hurt in a twelve-year-old is one thing, but even when we get older, we don't really get much better, do we? We may have become a little tougher, but we're just as quickly and easily disappointed as when we were children.

The disappointments of childhood are mostly of the trifling kind, yet there are other types of disappointment that are quite serious. So what should we do when such things occur? The answer, child of God, is to hear Him when He says, "This thing is from me." Believe this in your grief, and the day will come when you'll believe it in your joy. Believe it in your tears, and the day will come when you'll believe it with your smile. For what is a disappointment to you could be God's *appointment* for you.

Heavenly Father, thank You for all the things that have happened to me to show me how weak I am and how much I need your grace and mercy. Your strength is the only thing that gets me through each day. I praise and thank You. In Jesus' name I pray, amen.

ALL THE WAY MY SAVIOR LEADS ME

All the way my Savior leads me—
What have I to ask beside?
Can I doubt His tender mercy,
Who through life has been my guide?
Heav'nly peace, divinest comfort,
Here by faith in Him to dwell!
For I know, whate'er befall me,
Jesus doeth all things well;
For I know, whate'er befall me,
Jesus doeth all things well.

All the way my Savior leads me—
Cheers each winding path I tread,
Gives me grace for ev'ry trial,
Feeds me with the living bread.
Though my weary steps may falter
And my soul athirst may be,
Gushing from the rock before me,
Lo! a spring of joy I see;
Gushing from the rock before me,
Lo! A spring of joy I see.

All the way my Savior leads me—
Oh, the fullness of His love!
Perfect rest to me is promised
In my Father's house above.
When my spirit, clothed immortal,
Wings its flight to realms of day,
This my song through endless ages:
Jesus led me all the way;
This my song through endless ages:
Jesus led me all the way.

Fanny Crosby (1875)

— 8 —

HOW THE DEVIL USES
RELIGION TO ATTACK US

*Then all the tax collectors and the sinners drew near to Him
to hear Him. And the Pharisees and scribes complained, saying, "This Man receives sinners and eats with them."*

Luke 15:1–2

There are two kinds of sinners: the religious sinner and the
nonreligious sinner. Among the people of Jesus' day were four
classes: publicans, sinners, Pharisees, and scribes. Though
all were, in fact, sinners, the Pharisees and scribes didn't
know they were, while the publicans and sinners did know.

It's most significant that one of the greatest conflicts
Jesus experienced while walking the earth was with religious
people, and if you press further, you will find that Jesus'
conflict was with the Orthodox set. You'll find in the New

Testament a sharp line of demarcation being drawn, with the Lord Jesus on one side and His enemies on the other.

In the day in which we live, when we think of a conflict of Jesus with His enemies, we might picture Jesus on the same side with fundamentalist church people, presidents of Bible institutes and professors of homiletics, good church workers and board members, evangelists, pastors, and the like. Over on the other side might be the liberals and those who run saloons, gangsters and juvenile delinquents, harlots and thieves.

This seems clear enough. The only trouble is, it isn't true. When our Lord Jesus Christ was on earth, here was the division: On one side stood Jesus, and beside Him were the harlots; the publicans and pagans; those who couldn't walk, see, hear, or speak; the sick and infirm people. Over on the other side stood the rulers of the synagogues and the fundamentalists, the Pharisees and the church workers, the canters and those who read the Law of Moses daily or weekly in the synagogue.

So when Jesus Christ came down from heaven's pure glory to walk among us, that unsullied soul of His who never knew the faintest shadow of wrong thought, the only enemies He found were not only religious people but *His* religious people. His enemies were the Jews and His people who expounded the Scriptures rightly. Jesus did not rebuke their doctrinal positions. He did not correct them by saying, "You don't teach the Scriptures like you should." He didn't say that, for His enemies were good expounders. They were the conservators of orthodoxy, and the ones where righteousness should have dwelt. Nevertheless, referring to Jesus, they said, "This man receives sinners."

These religionists hounded Jesus until finally they put Him where they had planned to put Him from the beginning—on a Roman gibbet. And there He hung, blood streaming down His side and running off His feet onto the rocky ground. And those who hung Him there were not the pagans, not the harlots, not the publicans; they were the scribes and the Pharisees and the high priests. The good and moral people. Religion without love is a dangerous thing.

The religionists said, "Listen to this blasphemer. He claims that if we destroy the temple, He will raise it up in three days." And in their self-righteousness they didn't see that Jesus was proclaiming to the people that God had given them himself as an everlasting temple. "This temple is," He said, "my body, and someday you're going to destroy it on the cross, and in three days it's going to be raised again from the dead, and I'm going to come out of the tomb. I will establish eternal life and bring it to light through my gospel, so that all the dying world can live forever if they repent and believe in me, and all those marked with mortality shall become immortal." They will rise from the dead just as He rose from the dead. But the religionists didn't know that was what He had meant, so they took Him out and nailed Him to a cross to die for claiming He was going to raise up the temple in three days' time.

Jesus' healing of the sick on the Sabbath day also went against the religionists of His day. Jesus didn't mind stopping to heal people on the Sabbath. Our Lord was so informal, so completely relaxed and at ease, that He reached out to those in need spontaneously and without fanfare. There were no programs printed and distributed to advertise His miraculous works, and nobody knew exactly what would happen. Yet love was at work. Love was walking around on the earth—healing, blessing, teaching, admonishing, drawing the people to himself, those who had ears to hear (Matthew 11:15; Mark 4:9).

And when He came to the sick or He noticed someone suffering, He healed them. The Pharisees said, "We can't stand this. It's against our tradition. It's contrary to the laws of our fathers." They glared at Him while He made others' pain disappear, and they glared at Him while blind, milky eyes were suddenly filled with light, and the healed person saw for the first time the blue sky above and the green grass below. They said, "We can't have this. If this man continues to heal on the Sabbath day, He will disrupt our constitutional setup, and we will lose our influence among the people if we don't arrest Him soon." They had to bide their time, though. They couldn't kill Jesus right away because they were afraid of the public's reaction. But as soon as they could get to Him, they crucified the man who had reached out and loved people, healing and restoring them one by one.

Many through the ages have glorified Jesus because He loved people. And if He loved people, I want to love people. Of course, loving others doesn't mean being a soft, mousy, smiling fellow. The Pharisees loved people technically and legally, while Jesus truly loved them. He walked among them and healed them. In fact, loving people was more important to Him than were principles, laws, and regulations. In all the wide world today, there are those who can thank Him that He loves people, that He loves plain people, sick people, tired people, old people, and bereaved people.

Another reason the religionists despised Jesus was because He exposed their hypocrisy. With love in His heart, the Lord saw through all the religious leaders' little schemes. He saw how they walked around quietly, stroked their beards, prayed, and shook their holy phylacteries to awe the public and common people, displaying for everyone just how important they were.

Here were the learned rabbis in their religious garments. Their beards and hair were done up perfectly, and everything about them was impeccable, at least on the outside. But Jesus looked past their garments and saw the maggots crawling inside their hearts and the serpents squirming through their souls and the darkness in their minds. He approached the priests boldly and told them the truth of their condition before God.

The priests could not tolerate that because they might have to find different jobs of a lower status if Jesus exposed them for the hypocrites and scoundrels they were. This is what I call *priestcraft*, and it still exists today. You don't have to look to the Catholic Church to find it, for it's in Protestant churches as well. I pray that God will deliver us all from the hypocritical priestcraft within the Church.

When John saw Jesus in a vision, walking among the golden candlesticks, he noticed a belt around His waist, and on that belt he saw two keys. They are the keys to death and hell. Nobody else gets to have these keys: no church, no denomination, no school, no conference, no council, no college of cardinals, no bishops, no popes, no rabbis. So Jesus took the keys away from the priests and put it on His belt, and He opens heaven and hell as He wills for those who love Him and for those who reject Him. I'm glad about that, aren't you? Yet they crucified Him for those very charges I have mentioned.

These Pharisees said, "This man receives sinners." They made it an accusation and a charge against Him, and yet throughout the centuries people have praised Him for taking in sinners.

John Newton, D. L. Moody, and Augustine thanked God for His receiving sinners. We thank Jesus for what they cursed Him for and praise Him for what they crucified Him for. They nailed Him on a cross because He wouldn't agree that righteousness was an external thing and had to do with keeping the laws and rules. Rather, Jesus taught that righteousness was internal, a matter of the heart. So they used their laws and rules to have Him nailed on the cross. They said, "We will crucify this man because He dares to receive sinners." Then these actual sinners and hypocrites spat on Him. Jesus willingly went to the cross, bled, and died for the very persons who spat on Him.

It would serve us well to lower ourselves. Humility, repentance, self-examination, and fear of the Lord are dear in God's eyes. Wherever there is penitence, it rises like a sweet puff of incense into the nostrils of the Most High. Conversely, even one iota of superiority entering our hearts stinks in His holy nostrils. To be a righteous Christian and yet not be a self-righteous Christian is the work of the Holy Spirit. And if God doesn't work within us to make us humble, meek, and lowly, we are apt to kindle in our hearts that which the Pharisees and the scribes had. That terrible self-righteousness that didn't know God when they saw Him face-to-face. That frightening thing that would put words above deeds, and laws above people, and would crucify a man whose only crimes were that He loved sinners and healed the sick on a holy day.

He who with shining eyes would tell the world, "I come to bring you immortality, I come to take away sin." Those were His crimes. The religious leaders manufactured them. They paid lying men and suborned witnesses to lie about Him, but they could make nothing stick. The only crime they could level against Him was that He had claimed to be equal with God: "I and My Father are one" (John 10:30). But it was true. And I'm glad He is God. I can't put myself in the hands of anybody less than God.

As long as I keep my right mind, here are two knees that will never bow to man. But there is a Man whose name is Jesus, born of the Virgin Mary, who suffered under Pontius Pilate, was crucified, and rose from the dead on the third day to ascend to the right hand of God the Father Almighty, and from thence He shall judge the quick and the dead. That Man said, "I and My Father are one." I, for one, believe Him, and I will bow to Him.

O God, it is with fear and humility that I bow before Thee today. The enemy knows very well how to con me into some form of heresy. How I praise You that the Holy Spirit is guiding me each day in following You more faithfully and defending me from the attacks of the enemy. I pray this in Jesus' name, amen.

HE HIDETH MY SOUL

A wonderful Savior is Jesus my Lord,
a wonderful Savior to me.
He hideth my soul in the cleft of the rock,
where rivers of pleasure I see.

He hideth my soul in the cleft of the rock
that shadows a dry, thirsty land.
He hideth my life in the depths of his love,
and covers me there with his hand.

A wonderful Savior is Jesus my Lord,
he taketh my burden away.
He holdeth me up, and I shall not be moved;
he giveth me strength as my day.

He hideth my soul in the cleft of the rock
that shadows a dry, thirsty land.
He hideth my life in the depths of his love,
and covers me there with his hand.

With numberless blessings each moment he crowns,
and filled with his fullness divine,
I sing in my rapture, "Oh, glory to God
for such a Redeemer as mine!"

When clothed in his brightness, transported I rise
to meet him in clouds of the sky,
his perfect salvation, his wonderful love,
I'll shout with the millions on high.

He hideth my soul in the cleft of the rock
that shadows a dry, thirsty land.
He hideth my life in the depths of his love,
and covers me there with his hand.

Fanny Crosby (1890)

— 9 —

DISCOURAGEMENT: A VALUABLE TOOL OF THE DEVIL AGAINST CHRISTIANS

Look, the LORD your God has set the land before you; go up and possess it, as the LORD God of your fathers has spoken to you; do not fear or be discouraged.

Deuteronomy 1:21

I doubt that discouragement is the greatest enemy the Christian has, but it can easily be the greatest nuisance a Christian has to deal with. It is valuable to the devil in his war against us because it is seldom recognized for what it is.

When Christians become discouraged, common sense tells them they are just being realistic. We forget that it is not realism but discouragement, and it often works when no other temptation will. A Christian who would not be guilty of any sin willingly, and who has victory enough not to fall into temptation unwillingly, may yet be visited by this infernal dark shadow from the pit, which we call discouragement. And this greatly hinders the Christian life.

Discouragement can easily become a ruling emotion. It is more than an emotion; after a while, it becomes a disposition, an outlook, and an attitude, a darkened lens through which we view everything before us. The mood is the mental climate. It isn't the individual person so much as the weather on the landscape of their life, which has captivated the person. Just as the weather isn't the field or the farm, and yet it goes a long way in determining if the farm will yield a good crop or not. The mood is not the person, but it determines which and how many plants will grow. Joy, victory, and effective ministry can't grow in a climate of discouragement. Rather, what's often found are fear, self-pity, and self-absorption—preoccupation with one's own feelings, thoughts, or situation.

We would be surprised if we could somehow know the number of Christians who are bothered by a degree of discouragement, for it spares no one. It affects the young Christian as well as the old. After serving the Lord, more or less raggedly and spottily for a long two-thirds of a lifetime, I'm nevertheless as prone to discouragement today as I was when I was seventeen. If I'm an example, even a poor example, it is safe to say that discouragement spares nobody. The soberminded man you take to be a solid, self-assured person may well be suffering from a deep discouragement that affects him physically, mentally, and spiritually.

Then there are the radiant Christians—those shining, ebullient people among us who seem to overflow, and yet deep in their hearts they often get discouraged. They keep the shine on and don't mean to be hypocritical because they've learned to smile no matter what. But if you could get at the root of their lives, you would doubtless find that they are quite discouraged over something. Even the more down-to-earth Christians, those who are practical and measured in the way they approach life, can find themselves discouraged.

But what are the causes of such discouragement? The difference between negative preaching and positive preaching of the Bible is that negative preaching finds out what's wrong, whereas positive preaching prescribes the remedy. The doctor who diagnoses and tells you what's wrong, then sends you on your way is only half a doctor. A book that tells us what's wrong would be half a book, whereas a book that tells us what's wrong and then goes on to tell us what to do about it is a whole book.

One of the causes of discouragement is loneliness. Elijah is a dramatic example of a great man who became deeply discouraged because nobody around him understood him and nobody was going his way. He lacked the support of like-minded souls. It may be that in your home or office, or wherever you spend the majority of your time, that you have no like-minded souls with whom you can have fellowship.

Before getting to the cure, I want to let you in on a surprising fact: the loftier and more dramatic the character is, the further it can plunge into discouragement. There never was another man in his lifetime, or perhaps in a thousand years in Israel's history, who could have gone on to the mount and dared to call the prophets of Baal to test their god like Elijah did. He did that and then went from the mount where the fire fell and came straight down to the cave and the juniper tree in despair.

The higher up you can go, the further down you can go. There's a saying in the boxing ring that "the bigger they are, the harder they fall." That same thing is true in the spiritual arena, unless we look up and find the means of grace whereby we are lifted from the fog of discouragement. Some Christians are never discouraged because they never have much to aim at. They don't expect anything, and when they don't get it, they say, "Well, I didn't expect it anyway." But there are Christians with high ideals, which may turn them back on themselves in discouragement. The loftier the ideals and the spiritual aspirations, the wider we are open to the invasion of discouragement.

So then what is the cure? The cure is to remember that your discouragement is based upon an error. You think you're alone when you are not. In the first place, there are thousands of others like you. Our culture makes clubs of all sorts. There are marriage clubs, redheaded clubs, and bald-headed clubs, so why shouldn't we form a little club of those prone to be discouraged and talk it out with each other? Surely you'd find that there are a lot of people like you, those who have struggled with discouragement. If they told the whole truth, they'd remind you that there were times when they felt pretty blue about this whole business of serving God in an evil world. So you're not alone, and your discouragement is based on a failure to remember that God is with you every moment of your life.

Keep that in mind—you're never by yourself. Are not the angels sent forth to minister to those who will be heirs of salvation? But you might say, "Yes, that's all right for the saints: St. Teresa and St. Francis, Finney and Spurgeon. The angels no doubt helped them. But not somebody like me." What kind of mother would give all of her attention to her healthy, strong children and let the sick ones lie and suffer? What kind of God would God be if He sent His angels to bless Augustine and Julian and forgot about us poor people who are in such great need? No, He sends His angelic ministers to minister to them who will be heirs of salvation but who, for the moment, are in a tight spot.

When our Lord was praying in the garden and sweating blood, the angels came and ministered to Him. It was not when He was in Joseph's carpenter shop, helping his father and growing up to be a big boy; that wasn't when he needed the angels. It was when blood was flowing from his pores, sweat as blood. If you're discouraged, you're the one the Lord has pointed out. When Elijah was stuck in deep discouragement, so deep that as he went to sleep, blue and despondent, God said to an angel, "Go down and feed Elijah the prophet." The angel went down and baked cakes for Elijah—not for a radiant, victorious prophet, but for a discouraged and despondent prophet.

Another thing that may discourage Christians is the wickedness of people. We have Jeremiah as our biblical example. Jeremiah looked around, and everywhere he looked he saw wickedness. There were no newspapers at the time, but if there had been, Jeremiah would have found the front page covered with reports of wicked deeds and schemes. Jeremiah got tired of talking because he didn't have anybody paying attention to him. He got so discouraged that he came to be called the "weeping prophet."

The stars in the yonder heavens don't shine in the daytime because there's already light upon the earth. So why do they shine at night? Because the darkness makes them visible. In all the periods of history that have been reasonably decent, the great saints have not stood out; they've always stood out when the darkness was upon the earth.

When our Lord came, there was darkness upon the earth. The Church burst into paganism as into the deepest hellish darkness. The Wesleys came, not when everybody was praying, but when nobody was praying except a little handful called the holy club. More than two thousand and six hundred years have passed since Jeremiah prayed and preached while in discouragement. Believing men and women have since learned how to live and shine in the darkness. They learned it from Jeremiah, who was discouraged so much of the time.

Captivity can also discourage us. Have you ever felt as though you were a captive? Do you ever shrug cynically when you hear somebody talk about our free American way of life and say to yourself, "Free? How do I become free?" There are those who get up and go to their jobs, punch the card, hear the bell ring, punch it out again, then go home and back. It's a repetition of in and out, up and down, day in and day out until you're utterly exhausted. The two-week vacation they give you doesn't help because you take your work with you and carry it back. You're a captive. And if you end up with any money left after you pay your bills, you have to pay it out in income tax. Or maybe somebody needs an expensive operation you have to pay for. Whatever the case may be, you certainly don't feel free.

Like you, the prophet Ezekiel was captive and sitting among the other captives by the River Chebar. Think about what this young prophet of Israel must have been thinking as he sat there despondent, knowing he was now a captive, an enslaved person in a strange land. But do you know what Ezekiel saw while he was a captive that he didn't see before? He saw heaven open and had visions of God. It's right from where we are in our captivity that we see such things.

The fellow who gets his way is not likely to be looking for God's way, but when we have our own way taken from us, we get a feeling of discouragement. But out of that, and through it all, the light of heaven may shine.

Then there's the gloom that comes from others, thus making our hearts discouraged. When Israel was entering the Promised Land, their fellow Israelites discouraged their hearts by saying that the people there were greater and taller than them. Half my life has been spent reassuring people that the Anakims aren't bigger than us. They may rate higher and weigh more, but they're not as big as we are in God. Nobody is as big as a Christian walking in the will of our Father. He's bigger than anything you can bring against Him anytime. "What then shall we say to these things? If God is for us, who can be against us?" (Romans 8:31).

I meet so many gloomy brethren, always anticipating something bad happening. Usually what they fear doesn't happen, but still they think it's going to. Do you know the answer and the cure for the gloom that is shed upon us by discouraged Christians? "My Presence will go with you, and I will give you rest" (Exodus 33:14). That's what God said to Moses when the brethren didn't want to fight the Canaanites. If the presence of God is with you, of whom should you be afraid?

This next source of discouragement may surprise you. Another thing that discourages people, if they're conscientious, is reading Christian biographies. If we read a Christian biography in the wrong way, it may harm us instead of helping us because of comparing ourselves with them. Soon we begin to wonder if we're Christians at all, and we get very down as a result.

One of the biographer's obligations that's owed to the public is to tell the whole truth. For instance, I told the whole truth about A. B. Simpson in the book *Wingspread*. Some readers huffed and puffed, saying, "You've sold him short." I didn't sell him short because, though he was a saint, he was a mighty human saint. There has never been a saint who didn't have a human side. We don't have to dig around for a weak spot; we will find them naturally.

Have you noticed that a biography from the Bible always helps? That's because God's Word doesn't cover up the human sides of the saints. The biographies in the Bible tell the whole story.

David stole Uriah's wife, Bathsheba, and murdered Uriah to cover it up. Those facts would probably be left out of your typical biography on the bookshelf, but not one the Holy Spirit wrote. If we can learn the whole story about a person, warts and all, we will be more encouraged than if we only read about the proudest moments of their experience.

What's the right way to think about biographies, so that we don't read about St. Francis and others and say to ourselves, "If that man is a Christian, I am nothing." First, we need to consider the whole story, and secondly, remember that the person you're reading about is dead. If A. B. Simpson were to come back to life and appear, I'd promptly shrink down to the size and height of his shoes. But as God's Word says, "a living dog is better than a dead lion" (Ecclesiastes 9:4). So even though you're not as mighty a soul as Holy Ann, you're alive, and she's dead. After nearly forty years of history in my little church, we've gotten to the place where we get misty-eyed and nostalgic as we talk about the great souls we once had in our fellowship. But they've gone to heaven and can no longer win a soul. They can't teach a class, and they can't do what they're called on to do. They're gone now.

If God depended on the dead saints, His work would grind to a sudden, terrible halt, and all the churches would fall apart. God takes what He has available, and that is you and me. We're all God has, so instead of being discouraged, trust Him and pray, *Father, I thank You that, although I may not be as faith-filled as the great souls of the past, I nevertheless love You and want to serve You.*

Now, consider these words: "For the LORD God will help Me; therefore I will not be disgraced; therefore I have set My face like a flint, and I know that I will not be ashamed. He is near who justifies Me; who will contend with Me? Let us stand together. Who is My adversary? Let him come near Me. Surely the LORD God will help Me; who is he who will condemn Me? Indeed, they will all grow old like a garment; the moth will eat them up. Who among you fears the LORD? Who obeys the voice of His Servant? Who walks in darkness and has no light? Let him trust in the name of the LORD and rely upon his God" (Isaiah 50:7–10).

If you've been stepping through shadows and darkness, and the devil or your enemies have threatened you, you have every right to stand up and say, "The LORD God will help me; therefore I will not be disgraced." Then hear God say, "All of you who walk in darkness and have no life, trust in the name of the LORD and rely upon your God, and you'll be all right." I believe that's true of you and me.

O God, there are times when, instead of focusing on You, I focus on myself, which only brings discouragement. Lift me out of this slough of despondency and give me Your perspective on my walk with You and on my fellowship with other believers. In Jesus' name I pray, amen.

NEVER ALONE

I've seen the lightning flashing
and heard the thunder roll.
I've felt sin's breakers dashing,
trying to conquer my soul.
I've heard the voice of Jesus,
telling me still to fight on.
He promised never to leave me,
never to leave me alone.

The world's fierce winds are blowing,
temptation's sharp and keen,
I have a peace in knowing
my Savior stands between.
He stands to shield me from danger
when earthly friends are gone.
He promised never to leave me,
never to leave me alone.

No, never alone,
No, never alone,
He promised never to leave me,
never to leave me alone.

No, never alone,
No, never alone,
He promised never to leave me,
never to leave me alone.

Ludie D. Pickett (1897)

—10—

THE MISTAKES OF ISRAEL
AND POSSIBLY OURS

Israel empties his vine;
He brings forth fruit for himself.
Hosea 10:1

Hosea was sent to Israel during one of the nation's times of declension. *Declension* is a nice word for backsliding, and that's what Israel did. The Israelites had forgotten some vital things: their origin in the covenant of Abraham and, in large measure, the God of their fathers. According to this prophet, Israel had a divided heart; and wherever there is a divided heart, there is a civil war. Jesus said, "Every city or house divided against itself will not stand" (Matthew 12:25). A divided heart means civil war within what John Bunyan called the little kingdom of man's soul. Jesus also said, "You cannot serve God and mammon" (Matthew 6:24), and Israel was trying to serve God and mammon. They had not quite dared to reject Jehovah, but they were putting up other altars and serving other gods as well.

That's called being double-minded, and James warned about it in his book (1:8). Jesus said we were to have a "single eye," which means having one focal point at which the eyes look. According to Hosea 9:4, Israel had put itself in a position where God rejected their offerings. The prophet said Israel was an empty vine, and so she brought forth fruit unto herself.

What's the purpose of a vine? It is to bring forth fruit for others. The fruit of the vine is never brought forth for the vine itself. The fruit of the vine is a gift from God, and the vine receives it as a gift for others. Israel's mistake was that they brought forth fruit for themselves. The vine is to bring forth fruit to be the food of the people and the food of other creatures and for the creation of other vines. Every grape has two or three seeds capable of producing other vines, so any given vine that produces fruit receives sweetness, fragrance, and nourishment from God so as to be given to others. Israel was backslidden in that they produced fruit and consumed it only for themselves. This was true of Israel then, but it's also true of many churches and many Christians now.

Many who claim to be God's children are doing the same today. Just like with Israel, when Christians keep their treasures for themselves, the vine becomes empty. There's something wrong with the vine when, instead of the gifts of God externalizing and flowing out into fruit for others and for the production of other vines to come, the vine stays within itself and is left with nothing but leaves and no fruit. The vine has missed the will of God and lies empty.

Our lives can become wholly selfish. Good, honest Christian people, without knowing it, can little by little become completely selfish so that it's all inflow and no outflow. The Lord Jesus said, "You shall receive power when the Holy Spirit has come upon you; and you shall be witnesses to Me . . ." (Acts 1:8). "He who believes in Me . . . out of his heart will flow rivers of living water" (John 7:38). What you receive, you do not receive for yourself.

If the Lord's people could only remember that we are not like the Dead Sea, which receives always and gives nothing off except what is taken away by evaporation. We are channels to give. We are neither lakes nor lagoons. He did not say "when the Holy Spirit comes, you'll be like a lagoon." He said "when the Holy Spirit comes, you'll be like a river," and rivers are always flowing. That is why you can pollute a pond, a lagoon, or a little lake, but it's very hard to pollute a river. There was a saying back among the hills of Pennsylvania where I grew up: "If water flows over two stones, it purifies itself." That may have been overstated, but that was the way we boys decided whether we could drink from a stream we happened upon. The river stays clean by nature of it always flowing. And that is the purpose of the Church: to be a river of living water for others.

What is the Church? Simply put, it is Christians working together toward a common goal. A local church is a place where Christians gather, you and me in a congregation, where we worship the Lord and seek to honor Him by doing His will here on earth. But sometimes churches don't do what they are supposed to. Too often we are like vines

103

that should bring forth fruit to be shared with others, but instead we keep it all for ourselves. As long as we refuse to inconvenience ourselves, being overly concerned about safety and comfort, we bring forth fruit unto ourselves. Thus we become centered on ourselves.

What's the cure for this? It's found in Hosea 10:12, which says, "Sow for yourselves righteousness; reap in mercy; break up your fallow ground, for it is time to seek the LORD, till He comes and rains righteousness on you." We want God to roll over us with huge waves of emotion, but that doesn't solve the problem. Emotion may compel a person to apologize to another and ask forgiveness. Everybody has a good cry and then goes back to their idols and back to their selfishness and back to their carnality. No, there's only one way to actually repent: to reverse our ways. Instead of going the way we've been heading, we turn and go the way we ought to go.

Jesus told a story about two boys and their father. The father said to them, "Boys, go work in the vineyard today." One of them flared up and replied, "I won't go." The other said, "All right, Father, I'll go," and then he went fishing. Then the boy who got angry and said "I won't go" saw sadness and hurt on the father's face. Minutes later, he was down on his knees, praying, "Oh, God, what a scoundrel I was." He got up and went straight out into the vineyard and worked all day. The father returned and found that the boy who said he would go, didn't, while the boy who said he wouldn't, did. Jesus said that is what repentance looks like. It's the actions, not the words, that matter most. We might say, "Let's meet and pray all night." (Yes, Father, we'll work in your vineyard.) But the next day, nothing about us has changed; we didn't meet, and we didn't pray.

Let's reverse our ways of selfishness and bring forth fruit not unto ourselves but unto others.

The prophet Hosea warned Israel about their bringing forth fruit unto themselves. God had given them the sunshine, the soil, the rains—they had everything they needed. But they turned in on themselves and failed to give what they had received to others: the poor and the weary and the friendless. God wants us to keep pouring out of our lives the resources He's lavished upon us—our love, time, energy, money—until, instead of saying the Church brings forth fruit unto itself, it can be said that the Church brings forth fruit to the ends of the earth.

I praise Thee, Lord, that You are bigger than my mistakes. I bow before You, seeking Your forgiveness and inviting You to be the utmost authority in my life. May my life bring forth fruit for those who are around me. In Jesus' name I pray, amen.

AMAZING GRACE

Amazing grace! How sweet the sound
that saved a wretch like me!
I once was lost, but now am found,
was blind, but now I see.

Through many dangers, toils and snares
I have already come;
'tis grace has brought me safe thus far,
and grace will lead me home.

The Lord has promised good to me,
His Word my hope secures;

He will my shield and portion be
as long as life endures.

Yes, when this flesh and heart shall fail,
and mortal life shall cease,
I shall possess, within the veil,
a life of joy and peace.

The earth shall soon dissolve like snow,
the sun forbear to shine;
but God, who called me here below,
will be forever mine.

When we've been there ten thousand years,
bright shining as the sun,
we've no less days to sing God's praise
than when we'd first begun.

John Newton (1779)

—11—

HOW THE DEVIL MANIPULATES THE PLAGUE OF THE HEART

Whatever prayer, whatever supplication is made by anyone, or by all Your people Israel, when each one knows the plague of his own heart, and spreads out his hands toward this temple: then hear in heaven Your dwelling place, and forgive, and act, and give to everyone according to all his ways, whose heart You know (for You alone know the hearts of all the sons of men), that they may fear You all the days that they live in the land which You gave to our fathers.

1 Kings 8:38–40

The word *plague* is one of the most terrifying words in the world. Since the dawn of history, this word has stopped us in our tracks. We read in history books about the black plague of the fourteenth century, a strange and mysterious thing that dropped on healthy people as if out of nowhere and struck them down. In the city of London alone, half the population perished. In fact, so many succumbed at once that the living couldn't bury all who had died of the disease.

In more recent times, we suffered the terror of the bubonic plague. It was spread by vermin, a louse on the bodies of rats. These rats would come from other countries and run over the ropes of the ships to the wharf. The bubonic plague is still a terrible disease to be reckoned with in medical circles.

In the Bible, plagues were curses that struck men and women with sores and spots, ending in a fatal disease. Plagues seemed sudden and mysterious, and it was horrifying to discover them. The Law of Moses included a plan and method for dealing with plagues. If someone came forward with a spot on their body, they were immediately isolated from everyone else except for a few, who carefully watched over the one affected.

But I want to talk about something even worse than plagues of the body. Let's talk about sin, which is a plague of the heart. I am not speaking of the masses here. One of the neatest ways to get out from under conviction is to focus on the masses rather than the individual. If we refer to a whole congregation, then it seems as though we can all rest. But when the Holy Spirit aims the light on you alone, and His sharp finger points to your heart and He says, "You are the one," then we can begin to get somewhere.

The Scripture says that every person should know the plague of their own heart. It's the most important thing to be dealt with today, or any day since the time of Adam and Eve, because Satan would be perfectly helpless if it were not for sin. The devil could never hurt anybody were he not in possession of the individual human heart. Jesus had nothing in Him that belonged to the devil. Meanwhile, the devil paced back and forth like a hound dog outside the Lord's door, wanting in. Jesus was perfectly safe as long as nothing belonging to the devil entered His heart.

It is the plague of the heart that makes the devil so destructive. It is the lever by which the devil can control a person.

I don't want you to pity yourself because you have been taught that sin is a disease. If it is a disease, we are to be pitied, not blamed. While the Bible uses the word *plague*, it is a figure of speech that teaches us how to deal with Satan. But the plague of sin is not accidental; it's not something of which I am an innocent victim. We often love and choose evil, which makes us responsible to God for the plague of our own hearts.

People will not end up in hell because Adam sinned. They will end up there because *they* sinned. They chose sin and loved it and knew the judgment of God against such things, and yet they continued to practice those things knowingly and willingly.

This plague of the heart is a bent within us to do evil. This proneness to wander is the most fatal and deadly of all enemies, more to be dreaded than any disease. Cancer can kill your body, but it can't touch your soul. But the plague of sin gets into your soul; it's more terrible than war or the atom bomb. The plague of the heart can destroy a whole man or woman for this world and for the world to come. It isn't something we can remove ourselves. We can't reduce sin to a thing, incarnate and materialized, and then operate on it. If so, everybody would be waiting in line outside the surgeon's office.

Sin is an attitude, a bent, a will, a choice, and an affinity. You can't get at that with a surgeon's scalpel. I can't get at your heart. If you have a plague in your heart, only God can handle that. No school or institution in the world could touch it. No preacher, evangelist, singer, or missionary could get to the plague of your heart because you are the lord of your own heart. You are the master of your fate, and God will not allow anybody else to change it.

Psychiatrists can't get at your heart, and even if they could, most of them don't know about the plague. This plague's power lies in the fact that people don't know it's there; then suddenly it spreads and overflows into your whole nature and ruins your conduct and your habits and finally your life itself.

It's a strange accompaniment of this plague of the heart we call sin that hardly anyone will admit its presence. We can get a whole congregation to stand and say, "I believe that all people have sinned," but then ask them to sit down and admit individually their own specific sins, and they become silent. We can shout the truth to the rafters and wait for reactions. Still they remain silent, not wanting to take personal responsibility. But if everybody stands together, we all save face. Everybody can say, "Well, I'm no worse than my brother on my right and my sister on my left, and the deacon that is behind me, and probably no worse than the pastor in the pulpit. So we're in good company." It's a sneaky way of escaping responsibility for our own sins.

Everybody's asking, "What's the matter with Christianity?" I'll give you an answer: We have made Jesus Christ into a joy-bringer and a back scratcher. We have forgotten that He came into the world to save us from the plague of our own hearts, and He saves each person individually. You can't go to God in groups, families, squadrons, or regiments. Each person goes alone, individually, and if a hundred people were to go to an altar to seek a clean heart, each one would have to go in utter loneliness of spirit. You must go to God completely alone as if He were in the desert or in a cave.

There are two concepts I want to emphasize. One is the cleansing of the forgiving love of God. The forgiving love of God sweeps in like a detergent and takes out all the sticky grease of iniquity. And the other concept is the restoration of moral innocence. Even though you know you have sinned, somehow by the mystery and miracle of the Lamb's blood, you've had moral innocence restored to you again. Restored Christians will not likely elaborate on what they were saved from because they are brand-new people.

Cain was a sinner, and he had a plague in his heart. I suppose when Cain and Abel were growing up, they used to play together, and sometimes Cain would pick his little brother up and carry him over the rough spots. And Cain likely kissed his mother good-night and greeted his father each morning. Cain was probably an average man, yet he had a plague spot in his heart that he didn't admit to. One day he went out to give an offering to the Lord alongside his brother, and the fire came down and consumed Abel's offering, but it didn't consume Cain's. Then that which had been dormant suddenly leaped up like a fire, and Cain became jealous and angry. Filled with hate, he turned on that brother with whom he had slept and eaten and played on the grass many times. He turned on that brother, beat him to death, and buried him in the leaves.

Cain couldn't have looked all that different from Abel. They had the same genes and the same parents. In fact, you might not have been able to tell them apart. In other words, it wasn't their appearance on the outside but what was going on in their hearts that made the difference. Cain had a plague spot in his heart, but he never went to God about it. So he skipped the blood and offered plants instead. But plants can't cleanse and cure the plague spots in our hearts; only blood can do that.

Remember Achan? When the Israelites destroyed Jericho and the walls came tumbling down, Israel was walking on air, filled with happiness over that mighty defeat. After Jericho had crumbled and fallen at the cries and shouts of the people of God, the Israelites marched over to Ai to do the same thing. Instead, they fled before the people of Ai, and thirty-six of their soldiers were killed. Joshua fell facedown and said, "O God, what happened that Israel turned her back before her enemies?" And God said, "I'll tell you what happened. Get up off your knees. There's a time to pray, and there's a time to do something, and the time has come to do something. You've got a plague spot in the camp, and that plague will go on to kill you unless you get rid of it." They found out who it was.

It was Achan. He was a man like Cain, a family man. He had a wife, and they had daughters. Achan was just like all the rest. In fact, he was so much like the rest of the people that they had to come up with a divine scheme to discover who had committed the sin. Achan was probably the kind of man whom his neighbors thought of as decent and responsible, a loving husband and father, but Achan had a plague spot in his heart. He was greedy. His love of money led him to take a Babylonian's garment when the opportunity presented itself.

It wasn't theft; it was disobedience. The garment didn't belong to anybody. But God had said "Don't touch anything," yet Achan touched it anyway. He took the gold and the silver and the garment home and buried them, hiding them under his tent. Joshua told Achan, "If I let you get away with this, this black plague will spread to all of Israel. You've got to die. Not only you, but your whole family." Achan didn't know that when he ignored the plague spot in his heart, it would result in the deaths of thirty-six soldiers, himself, his wife, and all his children. If he'd realized that, he'd have fled in horror.

Today we urge people to come to church and have their nerves relaxed. Come and have peace. Come and have happiness. Come and be sure you'll go to heaven when you die. What heretics we are. Jesus Christ died so we might be delivered from the plague of our hearts. That's what He died for. These other things, peace and joy and contentment, are mere byproducts of that one central truth.

Consider Ananias. Was he totally bad? No, Ananias was a decent fellow. We would have received him into our church and probably even elected him to the board. But Ananias was tempted in a moment. If he hadn't been caught when he needed the money, chances are he wouldn't have lied to the Holy Spirit. A person may live with this plague in the heart for half a lifetime, and it'll not embarrass them. Then one day it will catch you when you're not looking and destroy your life.

Ananias tried to get out of a tight spot by telling God he got paid less than he said he got paid and therefore lied to God. But he must have had some good in him or he wouldn't have been around with the rest of the Christians. They wouldn't have had a liar with them if they had known that's what he was. They did know, however, that lying was a plague spot in the heart, and if it were allowed to continue, it would contaminate the crowd. And in the end, they carried Ananias out.

I have deliberately named more colorful sins, but we don't have to be struck by an atom bomb to die. We can die of cystitis or an ingrown toenail. We can die in the most ignominious way possible. So you can end up in hell without being an Ananias, you can ruin your life without being an Achan, and you don't have to be as lost as Herod was. You don't have to murder someone to have a plague in your heart and die of it. The point is to figure out if you have this plague in your heart, then go before the Lord with it in repentance.

One evidence or sign of this plague in the heart is sexual sin. Those who indulge in lust and sexual sin are guilty of impurity in the body. Yet such people are no worse in the sight of a holy God than those who strut around proud of their purity, for their pride is a plague spot.

Resentfulness is another sign of the plague in the heart. Resentful people walk around with chips on their shoulders, holding tight to hidden grudges, always ready for a fight.

Anger or a bad temper is also a sign of the plague. Envy and jealousy are signs as well.

We can accept Jesus all we want, but if we don't acknowledge the plague in our hearts, we will never do anything about it.

God heals this plague of sin in three ways: blood, fire, and suffering. For some sins, when you become saved, the blood of Jesus Christ washes them away and you never have to deal with these sins again. For other sins, the fire of the Holy Spirit burns them away. But there are other sins that are so insidious and hard to locate, only deep suffering will expose them. There's a word I'd like to restore to our vocabulary, and that is *purgation*. The Church uses many familiar phrases: believe in Jesus; accept Christ; follow the Lord. These are lovely words, even if they've lost their meaning for a lot of people, but we need to bring back the idea and process of purgation—a purgation by blood and by fire. The Holy Spirit stands ready to burn away the plague in our hearts and wash them clean, yet each of us must recognize and admit to the plague in our own hearts.

For Jesus, and for the sake of righteousness, don't try to hide the plague in your heart behind a big successful Christian life. Instead, admit to it. If you say, "I'm a deacon in the church, it would be an awful shock to the congregation if I went forward to be delivered from an unclean heart," one of these days you will lose your temper and blow up like a small atom bomb and disgrace yourself in front of the church.

Don't gloss over a plague spot, no matter who you are. If you've got one, locate it now, then stretch out your hands to God. Let the blood of Christ and the fire of the Holy Spirit cleanse you and restore you.

O Lord, my sin is within me and so I come to Thee for cleansing. I acknowledge the plague in my heart and turn it over to You and trust You to deal with it in such a way that my life will bring praise and honor to You. In Jesus' name I pray, amen.

COME, THOU FOUNT OF EVERY BLESSING

Come, thou Fount of every blessing,
tune my heart to sing thy grace;

streams of mercy, never ceasing,
call for songs of loudest praise.
Teach me some melodious sonnet,
sung by flaming tongues above.
Praise the mount I'm fixed upon it,
mount of God's redeeming love.

Here I find my greatest treasure;
hither by thy help I've come;
and I hope, by thy good pleasure,
safely to arrive at home.
Jesus sought me when a stranger,
wandering from the fold of God;
he, to rescue me from danger,
bought me with his precious blood.

Oh, to grace how great a debtor
daily I'm constrained to be!
Let thy goodness, like a fetter,
bind my wandering heart to thee.
Prone to wander, Lord, I feel it,
prone to leave the God I love;
here's my heart, O take and seal it;
seal it for thy courts above.

Robert Robinson (1758)

—12—

THE DANGERS OF
ARROGANCE AND DEFEAT

*Though I also might have confidence in the flesh. If anyone
else thinks he may have confidence in the flesh, I more so.*

Philippians 3:4

The primary danger of arrogance and defeat is that the devil
knows how to use these attitudes to manipulate and control
the Christian. To see a Christian with the spirit of arrogance
is to see someone being controlled in some way by the devil.
Watch out for the danger of arrogance. Jesus was the Lord,
but He didn't have an authoritarian attitude toward others.
If you become arrogant, presumptuous, and prideful over
your victory and success, He will chasten you painfully.

Our Lord Jesus Christ was a carpenter's son and spoke the
plain language of the common people of His time. Then one

day He rode into Jerusalem on a donkey over strewn palm branches and garments laid before Him, and a mob lined the streets on all sides. They shouted, "Hosanna to the Son of David! Blessed is He who comes in the name of the LORD!" (Matthew 21:9). There was success, recognition, and honor to whom honor was due. This kind of public acclaim could have led Jesus to say, "Perhaps the devil was right. Maybe I can be king of the world. Maybe my friends who wanted me to be king were right all along." He could have reached into the depths of His mighty power and become king overnight.

But he dismissed the donkey, walked into the temple, cleansed it, and then prepared himself to face the cross, torture, and death. He would not allow success of any kind to lead Him astray—away from His purpose and His Father's will.

This is true of spiritual success as well. If you make some strides forward in your Christian life, be careful you don't allow the sin of pride to enter your heart. Paul warned us of this in the book of Philippians, chapter three, where he speaks to those who think they have amounted to something, who think they have arrived spiritually.

Remember, people may praise you today and sing "Hosanna," but then the next day the same crowd may shout, "Away with this man. Crucify him!" The same people who thought you were worthy of acclaim today may turn their backs on you tomorrow. So don't give much thought to public opinion, nor should we think too much of any success we may enjoy due to our gifts. Rather, we must thank God for all that we receive, and then move forward in Him.

On the opposite side of the spectrum is the danger of defeat or failure. And sometimes pride can even turn into defeat. Remember the battle of Jericho and how the walls came tumbling down? Afterward, Israel became overconfident, misplacing their confidence in themselves instead of God as they were going up to Ai. They took along only a few thousand soldiers and said, "Look what we did at Jericho." But they hadn't done anything. God had done it all.

The Israelites must have thought that perhaps the wind from their horns had blown down Jericho's walls. But whatever their reasons, they assumed they were responsible for the walls coming down. So the next day, they decided to take Ai, thinking they were now in high gear. Nothing generates success like success, they believed. They went out with their chests puffed out and their heads held high and stood ingloriously before those of Ai. And thirty-five thousand died.

Defeat followed success. And just like that, defeat can plunge you into discouragement and take out your spirit, hope, and drive. Discouragement, incidentally, is hardly a sin, yet it can lead to any number of sins. And to discourage is to dishearten—that is, to weaken one's stomach for the Christian life.

I'm reminded of those powerful words from the play *Henry V* by William Shakespeare: "He which hath no stomach to this fight, let him depart; his passport shall be made and crowns for convoy put into his purse: we would not die in that man's company that fears his fellowship to die with us." The Bard talks about someone having no stomach for a fight, meaning the person has lost their zeal for the job at hand. It's like a sick person who has completely lost their appetite. That's discouragement.

And in the kingdom of God, the lack of victory, or a defeat or two, can drive us into a state where we have no stomach for anything. We might pray, but we don't really feel like it. We take it like food we don't enjoy. We go to church, but we don't care for the church. The worship is tasteless, the sermon boring, the whole thing faithless because we are disheartened and defeated, which is true of many of God's people.

People who are disheartened haven't lost eternal life, their relationship with God hasn't changed, and they are still His children. Christ is still pleading their cause at the right hand of the Father, and heaven is still their home. But for the time being they have lost their stomachs, as defeatism has gotten ahold of them. I've gone into churches where it was obvious that nobody expected anything to happen. And the result was exactly what you'd expect: nothing happened.

The danger of defeat is that it will bring with it defeatism, but keep in mind that it is never a disgrace to lose. It's when we allow our losses to build in our minds a psychology of defeat that this becomes dangerous. And such a thing can easily happen if we don't watch for it.

Say a person slips and falls on an icy sidewalk. Should that person just lie there and say, "I suppose there's no use in my trying again"? Or if the person were to struggle to their feet, but after walking half a block, fall again, they might very well say, "Something is seriously wrong with my equilibrium, and I'll have to accept myself this way. I can never walk upright on the ice again." In other words, defeatism is to allow one or more failures to place permanent failure in your heart. According to Proverbs 24:16, "a righteous man may fall seven times and rise again."

I met a young man at a conference whose chin was just about reaching the floor. I greeted him, but there was no response. He didn't smile or reply except to say, "Something awful happened to me. I just took my examination for ordination, and they won't ordain me." I told him, "Listen, Lincoln was defeated twice before he was elected. If God has called you, go to your examining board and find out what you didn't know, go to the library and study harder, then ask for another examination." The chin began to come up a little. I continued, "Don't allow a little thing like this to get you down. If God called you, He's not withdrawing that call just because there were some questions you couldn't answer. Study, figure out where you went wrong, and then ask God to help you." And that's exactly what he did. He's now one of our pastors and is getting along just fine.

Suppose you earnestly pray for something and don't get it; even if it's obvious you're not going to get it, don't let that discourage or defeat you. Maybe you need to reexamine your motives or change the way you're living. Maybe you've misunderstood the will of God. Go to the Scriptures, search them out, get right with God, and then try praying again and press on. Finally, the Lord may tell you, "You're praying for the wrong thing. Pray for this thing instead and you will see My blessing. But don't be defeated."

If, however, you are feeling quite defeated, here are some points to consider:

First, do not accept the judgment of your own heart about yourself because anybody's heart is bound to go astray, and a discouraged heart will for certain go astray. In other words, don't think about yourself the way you *feel* about yourself. Don't accept the testimony of your own heart. Go to God in Christ, remembering His unfailing love for you, and that Christ loved you enough to die for you. He thought you were worth something. If you're a Christian, the Holy Spirit dwells in you, and He hasn't turned you away.

If Gideon had accepted the judgment of his own heart, he never would have listened to God. He never would have experienced victory. Instead, he would have stayed in his depression, pounded out a few grapes, made a little wine and a little oil, and kept out of the fight. But God came to the defeated, discouraged Gideon and said, "Get up, you mighty man of God!" Gideon replied, "Did you mean me? Me, a mighty man of God hiding on the ground?" God said, "Yes, you. Get up, get up, get up." And Gideon accepted God's judgment of him. He went out and was victorious, putting the Midianites to flight.

Secondly, we should avoid making important decisions while we're discouraged. Never say yes or no to opportunities when you're down, because if you decide when you're discouraged, it will likely be the wrong decision. Don't resign from or accept a job when you're discouraged. Don't move or buy and sell property when you're down. Instead, go before God and seek His mind regarding any important decision, letting His grace shine into your heart as you ask Him to push away the dark clouds and give you the light of His countenance, to remove any feelings of defeat from your spirit. And when you can say, "I can do all things through Christ who strengthens me" (Philippians 4:13), and mean it, then you can make your decision knowing you're doing so in His will.

Thirdly, remember that failure, whether in business, your personal life, or any other circumstance, doesn't make you any less dear to God. I'm so glad God doesn't look at my circumstances to determine how much to love me. We sometimes judge people that way, but this isn't true of God. If you have failed in any way, this doesn't make God any less loving toward you and doesn't affect God's love for you. Neither does it affect His promises to you.

That brings me to the fourth thing you can do to avoid defeatism, which is to remember the promises of God. Go to the Bible and read each one of them until your heart begins to leap with joy. They're still good and true, even though you've suffered a defeat.

God is everything. Not success, not failure, but God. Not winning, not losing, just God. My victory can't enrich God, and my defeat can't impoverish Him. If I make good, I bring God nothing. And if I peter out, I don't take anything from Him. God is our rock and our fortress, our deliverer, our strength, and our high tower. He is sent from above, He rescued us, and He drew us out of treacherous waters. He delivered us from our strong enemy and from those who hated us. He brought us to a large, open place and delivered us because He delighted in us. We can hold on to this verse: "For You will light my lamp; the LORD my God will enlighten my darkness" (Psalm 18:28).

This poor little light of mine, maybe it's gone out, but God will light your candle for you once again and enlighten your darkness. God is our refuge, and we're not going to let victory spoil us or defeat us. We're going to take them both in stride. Win or lose, we're on God's side, and if we keep putting our trust in Him, we're winning whether we know it or not. That is faith.

Father, it is in the depth of my discouragement and failure that I begin to understand Your great love for me. You love me not because of what I do, but because of who You are. Thank you for your inexhaustible love. In Jesus' name I pray, amen.

THIS LITTLE LIGHT OF MINE*

The light that shines is the light of love,
lights the darkness from above,
it shines on me and it shines on you,
and shows what the power of love can do.
I'm gonna shine my light both far and near,
I'm gonna shine my light both bright and clear.
Where there's a dark corner in this land
I'm gonna let my little light shine.

On Monday he gave me the gift of love,
Tuesday peace came from above.
On Wednesday he told me to have more faith,
on Thursday he gave me a little more grace.
On Friday he told me just to watch and pray,
on Saturday he told me just what to say,
on Sunday he gave me the pow'r divine
to let my little light shine.

This little light of mine, I'm gonna let it shine.
This little light of mine, I'm gonna let it shine.
This little light of mine, I'm gonna let it shine,
let it shine, let it shine, let it shine.

Origin of song unknown

—13—

THE ROOT OF OUR SPIRITUAL WARFARE

Now the serpent was more cunning than any beast of the field which the LORD God had made. And he said to the woman, "Has God indeed said, 'You shall not eat of every tree of the garden'?"

Genesis 3:1

I hesitate to allow the outside world to define the devil for me. If we understand how the devil got started in the Garden of Eden, we can understand what he is doing now, because the Garden of Eden is the root of all the devil's actions throughout history.

Hollywood cannot and will not define or describe the devil for me. After all, he controls many of them. They view the devil in ways that are contrary to the Bible, and we risk being misled if we allow the world to define and explain spiritual ideas. Let's look instead at how the Bible describes the devil.

In Genesis 3, Satan comes to Adam and Eve in the form of a serpent. Given that God created the serpent, why did the devil choose this creature to get to Adam and Eve? We don't know. But we do know that after sin entered the world, unlike any other creature God had made prior to this, this "serpent" was cursed by God. In other words, this was the very first curse God uttered.

"So the LORD God said to the serpent: 'Because you have done this, you are cursed more than all cattle, and more than every beast of the field; on your belly you shall go, and you shall eat dust all the days of your life. And I will put enmity between you and the woman, and between your seed and her Seed; He shall bruise your head, and you shall bruise His heel'" (Genesis 3:14–15).

The devil's initial appearance did not reflect his true intention to harm Adam and Eve. He seemed so harmless in the beginning when in Genesis 3:1 he tried to tempt Eve, saying, "Has God indeed said . . . ?" This comes across as if he's not trying to get Eve into trouble or lure her into doing something bad. He knew a direct approach wouldn't work. Instead, he was merely questioning whether God's word was accurate. "Are you sure you can really trust God? Do you think God has your best interests at heart?"

Keep in mind that the Garden of Eden was a perfect place, and Adam and Eve were perfect, sinless human beings. It is evident, however, that the devil could infiltrate their territory and bring sin to humanity. How did this happen?

Everything in the Garden of Eden's environment was perfect. There was no rebellion anywhere against God the

Creator. Adam and Eve had a wonderful relationship with God. Genesis 2:25 states, "And they were both naked, the man and his wife, and were not ashamed." They were deeply rooted in their relationships with each other and with God, and nothing in their lives indicated that they had disobeyed God in any way. They were perfect in all aspects.

We have a hard time picturing Adam and Eve in this situation with no sin in a perfect place, a perfect partnership between them, with nobody else around who could endanger their friendship. Unlike the sinful world today where evil, disobedience, and heresy are commonplace, the relationships between Adam and Eve and God were pure and undefiled. So it's into this perfect world the devil came in the form of a serpent to introduce them to sin, and his plan of attack would have to be subtle.

The devil was not trying to convince Adam or Eve to commit what some would consider a "big sin." The devil's actions were designed to make Eve question the truth of God's words. This is where the devil begins. Initially, he doesn't tempt people to commit a murder, pull off a bank robbery, or some similar felony. These are the later effects of an individual's internal sin. However, if the devil could only get us to doubt the truth of what God has said, he would be exercising some measure of control over us.

The moment the devil convinced Adam and Eve they could become like God and possess all knowledge is when the human race began its precipitous fall into depravity. Satan presented Adam and Eve with what appeared to be a benign choice. They had to decide between God's words and Satan's words. Who were they going to believe? So they accepted the bait and were duped by Satan's deceit and evil intent.

The Bible teaches that God created us with enormous intellectual and spiritual potential. In God's likeness we were created. Sin was the culprit in destroying this potential, and sin is what gives us a sense of being orphans in the world. Letting sin enter our lives leads to the devil taking advantage of us and whispering his wicked lie into our ears, "You don't matter to God. He doesn't really care about you." Since the Garden of Eden, the devil has been successful at doing this. Over the centuries, nothing has changed in this regard as the enemy continues his attack on humanity with tenacity.

There is no doubt that the devil abhors our joy in the Lord and will use every means at his disposal to rob us of this holy joy. A Christian living in God's presence irritates the devil more than anything else, and once the devil wants something badly enough, he will stop at nothing to have his way.

The devil should never be trusted. Because the flesh is weak, even though the spirit is willing, we must always watch and pray in preparation for his attacks. There are some days when the devil tries to convince me that God doesn't care about me. God feels far away. But what I feel is irrelevant, for God's love has been demonstrated, and this cannot change; if it did, He would cease to be God. Therefore, I will not fall for the devil's lie that God isn't who the Bible says He is. We must remain rooted in God's Word.

Earlier, I mentioned a wonderful truth found in the Bible: The Almighty God has the power to use something intended for evil for good. It must feel like a cruel joke to the devil when he realizes that he can do nothing to alter God's sovereign will. In fact, he has never done anything without God's permission because it's only with borrowed power that the devil can act. The throne in heaven proclaims the supreme authority of the One seated there, and that is God Almighty himself.

When Joseph's father passed away, his brothers feared this would be a chance for Joseph to exact revenge on them for selling him into slavery. But Joseph told them, "But as for you, you meant evil against me; but God meant it for good, in order to bring it about as it is this day, to save many people alive" (Genesis 50:20). God frequently uses the enemy's actions, such as those in Joseph's life, to prepare the way for His amazing grace to be revealed. (I'm sure the devil is furious about this.) With that in mind, even though the Garden of Eden episode seems like a disaster, we must remember that it was not a surprise to God. He had prepared for this, and what happened in the Garden opened a pathway for Him to demonstrate His grace and mercy through His Son, the Lord Jesus Christ. We need to understand this grace to know what salvation is all about. And from the very beginning, God was preparing for the ultimate defeat of Satan.

Humanity fell because of Satan's deception and the sin that resulted in destroying within us that fellowship for which we were created. It left a void inside us. This destroyed relationship is what caused Adam and Eve to be expelled from the Garden, and this is still Satan's overarching strategy to this day. Nothing has changed; the devil and his tactics remain the same.

Adam and Eve's understanding of God started to fade the instant they embraced Satan's plan: "I will be like the Most High." Ever since then, as men and women have attempted to exalt themselves above God, they have fallen deeper and deeper into a downward spiral, leading to hell's very depths.

While Satan's strategy has remained the same, he is too cunning to be uniform. He usually attacks us where we least expect him to, so always be ready. Never assume you have him in the rearview mirror. We live in a world that the devil has seized control of and tarnished. While this is our Father's world, we currently reside in a time when Satan has temporarily taken control of it.

The plague that Satan has spread throughout the human race derives from disobedience and revolt, because when we responded to his temptation with "I will," we broke free from our normal state. We've strayed from where we belong. We should be in the Father's house, but we are currently in the devil's house.

Ever since hijacking the world, Satan and his allies have been engaged in conflict over it. But, as it says in the book of Revelation, Jesus Christ will return and establish His rule and His peace over the entire planet. Then Christ who was once crucified for humanity will cast Satan out of the world that is not rightfully his, and He will take it over. While there is hope in the end, in the meantime we must remember we're in a battle. We must also remember that God greatly desires our fellowship, for we are not orphaned children. We are His beloved children.

———

The primary target for the devil's fiery darts is the new believer. The devil knows that destroying them before they mature is the most effective method for getting rid of them. Anyone who puts their faith and trust in the Lord Jesus Christ is the greatest opponent the devil has to face.

Like a con artist, the devil enters a person's life grinning. If con artists were nasty, angry, and aggressive, they would never be able to get away with what they do. Their Ponzi schemes wouldn't work. No, they persuade people to believe and place their trust in them because of their sweet demeanor, upbeat speech, and encouraging words.

It is the same with the devil. He applies subtlety as he looks to plant the seeds of doubt and skepticism about God in our hearts. What should we do in response? We must submit ourselves to the authority of the Bible whenever we read it. The devil desires to undermine and contradict the validity of God's Word in our lives, so we need to approach the Bible with humility, reverence, and submission. This enrages the devil.

We must respond to God's Word with a "Yes, He means what He says, and I surrender my life to Him." When we do that, we can be confident that the devil, in utter annoyance, will flee as far away from me as he can. He wants to have control over my life, and if he can't have that authority, at least he can try to undermine God's authority. But as a believer, I won't let that happen.

I think of Job, who had a hedge around him to keep his family safe. Even Satan understood this protection existed and that Job was impenetrable without God's approval. We must remember that and not let the devil fool us, but instead view every difficulty we encounter as a chance for God's grace to manifest itself in our lives.

Understanding the environment of our spiritual warfare will help us be better equipped to deal with the enemy's fiery darts. We are not thinking rationally if we imagine the devil isn't keeping an eye on us. We must put into practice that which Paul taught us: "Therefore take up the whole armor of God, that you may be able to withstand in the evil day, and having done all, to stand" (Ephesians 6:13). While the devil is aware of our weaknesses and knows how to manipulate human beings, the power of God working in and through His children is infinitely greater.

I praise You, O God, for the tenacity of Your grace. I have often been tricked by the enemy to think of You as less than what You truly are. Forgive me, Lord. I want to refresh my soul in Your Word, so that it will give me the strength and discernment to see what the devil is up to. I give my life completely to You, and with Your help, I will never succumb to the devil's lies. In Jesus' name I pray, amen.

AM I A SOLDIER OF THE CROSS?

Am I a soldier of the cross,
A follow'r of the Lamb?
And shall I fear to own His cause,
Or blush to speak His name?

Must I be carried to the skies
On flow'ry beds of ease,
While others fought to win the prize,
And sailed through bloody seas?

Are there no foes for me to face?
Must I not stem the flood?
Is this vile world a friend to grace,
To help me on to God?

Sure I must fight if I would reign;
Increase my courage, Lord;
I'll bear the toil, endure the pain,
Supported by Thy Word.

Thy saints in all this glorious war
Shall conquer, though they die;
They see the triumph from afar,
By faith's discerning eye.

When that illustrious day shall rise,
And all Thy armies shine
In robes of vict'ry through the skies,
The glory shall be Thine.

Isaac Watts (1721)

—14—

THE WALL BETWEEN
US AND THE DEVIL

Be angry, and do not sin: do not let the sun go down on your
wrath, nor give place to the devil.

Ephesians 4:26–27

When considering the devil's role in our spiritual battle and
how he tempts us, it is important to remember that he is not
the only way we are tempted. Even for Christians, temptation is a part of life.

Abraham may be the best illustration of this. "Now it came
to pass after these things that God tested Abraham, and said to
him, 'Abraham!' And he said, 'Here I am'" (Genesis 22:1). This
verse refers to Abraham being asked to sacrifice his son Isaac,
which has to be the biggest temptation in all of Scripture. I
find it difficult to comprehend Abraham's emotions at the
time. For Abraham, his son Isaac was of utmost importance.

But let's back up and see how we got to this point. Old Testament readers are no doubt already familiar with the story of Abraham and Sarah and their waiting for the arrival of their promised son, Isaac. Sarah was well past the gestational age at this point. After a few years of growing restless, Sarah believed she could find a solution. To bear a child, Sarah gave her husband Hagar, her handmaiden. She believed that by doing so, she would please God. In Sarah's mind, Ishmael was born to Hagar as the child God had promised her through Abraham.

She made a decision that was contrary to what God had said. The Ishmaelites, who are typically thought of as Arabs, were the offspring that stemmed from Sarah's choice. Over the years, Israel went through many difficulties with the Ishmaelites.

Eventually, however, God gave Abraham a son through Sarah herself. And then when Isaac was around twelve years old, God presented Abraham with a choice. He asked him to sacrifice his son Isaac, making him choose between his son and God's Word. Abraham would have done anything not to have to place his son on that altar. I have a sneaking suspicion he didn't sleep well that night.

But the following morning, Abraham gathered his son and his companions, and they set out for the location God had designated for him. I'm sure the young boy was interested in finding out where they were going. How Abraham could ever make such a choice reveals his relationship with God. He followed through and took Isaac up the mountain, and once at the top, they built an altar. Then Abraham took his son, bound him with ropes, and placed him on that altar.

Though it's hard for us to imagine, Abraham then reached for his knife, walked over to his son, raised the blade, and prepared to stab him. But at that moment, God stopped him. "And Abraham stretched out his hand and took the knife to slay his son. But the Angel of the LORD called to him from heaven and said, 'Abraham, Abraham!' So he said, 'Here I am.' And He said, 'Do not lay your hand on the lad, or do anything to him; for now I know that you fear God, since you have not withheld your son, your only son, from Me'" (Genesis 22:10–12).

This encounter helped Abraham grow in his relationship with God and strengthened his resolve to hold fast to his faith. God used him in a profound way. It's also an example of what believers in Christ need to fight spiritual battles. Yes, we should celebrate our salvation. The Lord Jesus Christ, who died on the cross, rose from the dead on the third day, and He alone is the source of our salvation, which is available to all who believe, who repent of their sins and place their trust in Christ. However, for those who follow Him, that is just the beginning. We have a journey before us that ends in heaven.

Ishmael was the devil's choice, whereas Isaac was God's choice. We must choose one way or the other. As recorded in Matthew's Gospel, Jesus said, "No one can serve two masters; for either he will hate the one and love the other, or else he will be loyal to the one and despise the other . . ." (Matthew 6:24).

Our spiritual warfare depends on the choices we make in our lives. There is nothing in my life that God will not ask me to sacrifice. The enemy, on the other side, has a different perspective. He would have asked Abraham to throw a birthday party for Isaac and made a big spectacle of the promised son who had finally come. This is his enticing strategy—to do what we want to do anyway rather than what God is asking for.

Sometimes there is a battle like David vs. Goliath. David won that battle victoriously. But the battle with Bathsheba was a completely different kind of battle. It was a battle David lost, much to his disgrace. At the time it probably felt like a smaller battle, but it turned out it was more than David could handle. Many times it's after a huge victory that the enemy sneaks in and lays another trap for us that we were not expecting. So when we think we can handle anything, we put ourselves at the enemy's disposal.

Each battle every day matters. I can't live for the devil during the week and then go to church on Sunday and worship God—it's either all or nothing. God will not accept a percentage of your life. You cannot bribe God with your tithes or good intentions. When God tempts us, it's clear He's asking us to do something, and we have a choice to make. But when the devil tempts us, we are usually unaware he is tempting us.

I think the devil loves to engage us in battle. It's what he lives for. He knows that perhaps he ultimately can't win, but he also knows he can do some damage in the process. The entire agenda of the enemy can be boiled down to one objective: to embarrass God through some of His children. The devil thought he could do that with Job in the Old Testament, but what the devil did not know was that God was in absolute control every step of the way. Though the devil is allowed to get to us, he cannot ultimately harm us.

What is it that comes between the devil and us? If we can understand the answer to this question, we will see more victory in our lives. The only thing that can come between the devil and us is God. That's what happened with Abraham. God stepped in and stopped him when he was ready to plunge the knife into his son's body. Sometimes God waits until the very last moment, but He's in charge and He knows when and what to do. God has His way of carrying out His will in a person's life, and there are times that God will use the devil and his tempting power to accomplish His will.

Perhaps Job is the key character in the Old Testament. The devil did everything he could to tempt Job and pull him away from God. At one point, even Job's wife gave up and said, "Do you still hold fast to your integrity? Curse God and die!" (Job 2:9).

Job had to choose between his wife and God, and I am sure the devil was manipulating his wife at this point in the story. The devil often uses someone we love or admire to tempt us to disobey God at some level. I believe it is a difficult aspect of our Christian experience but one we need to realize and protect ourselves from. We need to take our families and loved ones and give them over to the Lord as Abraham gave Isaac over to the Lord. When we do, the devil cannot tempt us in this regard. That doesn't mean he's not going to try, but it does mean our sacrifice must be continual. Because I surrendered yesterday doesn't mean I don't have to surrender today. Surrendering is not a one-time experience but rather a lifelong one.

After Abraham offered Isaac on the altar, he never saw his son the same again. Every time he looked at him, he was reminded of the sacrifice he gave to the Lord. Isaac was no longer Abraham's son; rather, Isaac belonged to God. This is what must come between the devil and us. If God is to be between the devil and me, everything I have must be sacrificed and surrendered to God. That which I keep from giving over to God is that which the enemy can use to tempt me.

The apostle Paul said, "Neither give place to the devil" (Ephesians 4:27 KJV). We must understand that it's up to us whether to give place to the devil. The devil cannot do anything in our lives that we do not permit him to do. We must make sure not to leave a little space for him in anything we do. He does not need much space, just enough to squeeze into our lives. And sometimes that little space is hidden from our notice, and maybe the devil will hang around for days or weeks before he begins anything. He will then attack when we least expect it.

Instead of giving place to the devil, my concern should be to give place to God, making sure that God is in all of me, not just some of me. I must admit this takes a lot of work to do. When I think I've given God everything, I usually see something I have missed. That's what personal prayer is all about. Searching our hearts for any space that God does not inhabit. That His presence is all through my life every day of the week.

Keep in mind that the devil delights in feeding into a person's confidence in themselves. As we build up our self-confidence, the devil is willing to give credit to *self* so long as he accomplishes his objective. He will let us have anything we want so long as it doesn't interfere with his purposes. The devil wants me to think that I'm perfect, which makes me an open target for him.

So the only thing that can come between the devil and me is God. Not religion. Not doctrine. Not psychology. Nothing. In fact, the devil delights in using religion to accomplish his wicked purposes. James wrote in his book, "You believe that there is one God. You do well. Even the demons believe—and tremble!" (2:19). The demons know what is true and that God is real. But just because they believe doesn't mean they are saved and on their way to heaven.

Though of course I am for correct doctrine, doctrine must serve as my pathway into the very heart of God. I need to believe and even tremble, but in my belief, my heart will be transformed to the glory of God. If I am transformed by God, that makes the devil angry, and he wants to take it away from me. Unfortunately, he has been successful in doing this many times with many people.

Don't give the devil any space. Instead, fill your heart and life with God every day, all day and night. Remember the story of Abraham and his beloved son Isaac, who was a promise from God.

Heavenly Father, I praise Thee for Your protection in my life. I confess to succumbing to temptation, but I am so grateful that Your grace is sufficient to cleanse me of my failures. Help me to walk on that path that leads me away from the devil and into Your loving heart. In Jesus' name I pray, amen.

THY SOLDIER I WILL BE

The die is cast, my choice is made,
A soldier I will be;

141

Where Jesus leads I'm not afraid,
A soldier I will be.
In any clime, in any place,
E'en can I not my Savior trace,
To spread the news of Jesus' grace,
A soldier I will be.

I'll follow Thee, my Savior,
No matter where it be;
I'll follow Thee, my Savior,
O'er mountain, vale, or sea;
I'll follow Thee, my Savior,
You can depend on me:
In joy or pain, in loss or gain,
Thy soldier I will be.

In spite of sorrow, toil, or pain,
A soldier I will be;
I'll bear the cross, despise the shame,
A soldier I will be.
I know no color, class, or state,
But cry, "Repent, ere 'tis too late!"
And save lost souls from hell's sad fate,
A soldier I will be.

Until I draw my latest breath
A soldier I will be;
And when my eyes shall close in death,
A soldier I will be.
And when I reach those gates of pearl,
I'll sheath my sword, my colors furl,
Defiance at the foe I'll hurl,
A soldier I will be.

Anonymous (1922)

—15—

THE ULTIMATE
SPIRITUAL TEMPTATION

*Then Jesus was led up by the Spirit into the wilderness to
be tempted by the devil.*

Matthew 4:1

I make no claims of understanding the devil's thoughts at
the time of Jesus' temptation. Perhaps he reasoned that after
fasting for forty days and forty nights, Jesus was in His most
precarious position. The temptation in the Garden of Eden
has some elements in common with Jesus' temptation in
the wilderness. In both cases they weren't tempted to do
something sinful, but to question God's authority. "Has God
indeed said . . . ?" the devil asked Eve in Genesis 3:1. In other
words, he was challenging the reliability of God's Word.

There are several things we can learn from Jesus' wilderness temptation. For one thing, *if* is the first word in every

temptation directed at Him. *If* is a questioning word and can be seen as an attempt to plant a seed of doubt in Jesus' heart. Just like in the Garden of Eden where the devil attacked Eve when she was most vulnerable, we find he also attacked Jesus in the wilderness when the devil thought He was most vulnerable. Note the devil's first temptation to Jesus: "If You are the Son of God, command that these stones become bread" (Matthew 4:3).

Jesus was probably starving after having fasted for forty days and nights, and the temptation's foundation was an appeal to the flesh. We are susceptible to the enemy's temptation when the flesh reigns supreme in our lives.

The enemy sometimes understands us better than we understand ourselves, but when it came to Jesus, the adversary did not know Jesus as well as he thought he did. I frequently ponder why the devil began with this temptation—it seems small compared to the later ones—but sometimes the devil's temptations primarily serve to distract us before a bigger temptation sneaks up on us unnoticed. He thought he could trick Jesus with a loaf of bread. Jesus, of course, could not be tricked.

It's amazing how Jesus handled these temptations. Notice that the phrase "It is written" was used in response to each one of them, which shows that He didn't just express an opinion about the temptation the devil was offering Him. Instead, Jesus connected them to the Bible. He is relying on the fact that the Word of God, which does not change, serves as the foundation for His decisions rather than His circumstances, which constantly change. "Man shall not live by bread alone, but by every word that proceeds from the mouth of God," said Jesus in response (Matthew 4:4). That is to say, "My strength comes from God's words rather than from the things around me."

As mentioned in the previous chapter, challenges to God's Word are the main focus of the devil's temptations. In my opinion, many in the modern Church do not understand what God has said, and they are unaware of the central themes of the Bible. Instead, they rely on religious rites and rituals to get them through. But this will not do.

The devil, who knows the Word of God well, will use every means at his disposal to taint the Bible. Sometimes he only twists a small portion of it, but never forget that every lie is built on a twisted version of the truth.

Next, Jesus was taken by the devil into the Holy City, where he placed Jesus on the pinnacle of the Temple and said to Him, "If You are the Son of God, throw Yourself down. For it is written: 'He shall give His angels charge over you,' and, 'In their hands they shall bear you up, lest you dash your foot against a stone'" (Matthew 4:5–6).

This is a chance for Jesus to demonstrate that He is who He claims to be, the devil says; in other words, that He actually is God's Son. This would appear to be a fantastic way for Jesus to prove himself to the world. But the true motivation for giving in to this temptation would be to draw attention to himself, which is the sin of pride.

Similarly today, the devil may tempt us to perform a miracle, demonstrating our sincerity as Christians. Extreme representations of who we are as Christians appeal to us. We make a big deal of it by drawing attention to ourselves and positioning ourselves where everyone can see us.

Jesus responds to the devil, "It is written again, 'You shall not tempt the LORD your God'" (Matthew 4:7). Jesus fights fire with fire. He essentially says to the devil, "If you want to use the Bible against Me, then I shall use the Bible against you." But Jesus not only quotes it, He obeys it.

To persuade me to do something that God does not want me to do, the devil will use my own beliefs and Scripture verses against me. As mentioned earlier in this book, James makes a very intriguing statement in his epistle: "You believe that there is one God. You do well. Even the demons believe—and tremble!" (James 2:19). The demons believe what we believe, but the difference between them and us is simply that their lives have not been changed by what they believe. As a Christian, my beliefs in the Bible transform me. I don't just hold a belief because of what I've learned, I act on it. Likewise, many educated Christians are able to cite Scripture and provide doctrinal explanations, but none of it has actually changed their lives.

Sometimes throughout history, the devil has infiltrated the Church through a doctrinal porthole. The devil doesn't storm our churches shouting obscenities and daring us to curse God. That wouldn't work. Instead, he enters our churches sneakily through the doctrines we hold, his purpose being to twist them into something genuinely unbiblical.

For example, look at the various Christian denominations that exist today—a few hundred in the United States, and several thousand worldwide. Of course, the issue with denominations is that Pharisees eventually rule and control them. Anyone can split off and start a new church if they don't share their church's exact beliefs, and such an endeavor is the devil's delight. I believe I am correct in saying there won't be any denominations in heaven. I'm looking forward to the day when all that nonsense will be behind us.

———————

Christians are frequently tempted to give up when they face a challenge or trial that includes temptation. If you're a Christian, I'm sure you've experienced this. I know I have. It feels like it's not worth it, and so you're tempted to quit and leave God. "Clearly, God, you don't want me, so I'm done." To some extent, every Christian has arrived at that point. We forget that God is using these difficulties and temptations to teach us that self-confidence is risky and unreliable. And in that way, we can give the devil a bit of credit for all the temptations that have led us to discover God's amazing grace and love.

I'm reminded again of Joseph in the Old Testament and how his brothers made fun of him, sold him as a slave, and claimed he was dead to their father. If you follow Joseph's life, you will see that he moved from one prison to another and from hardship to hardship, until he was finally in the place where he could establish a connection with the government. When Pharaoh realized who Joseph was, he freed him from prison and appointed him as his deputy. Joseph was able to prevent an impending famine in Egypt, and eventually he got to the place where he was supposed to be. Then he gave us the famous quote about God using evil for His purposes (Genesis 50:19–20).

He entered that "place of God" as a result of all the temptations that were set before him in an effort to destroy him. But Joseph persisted, and the enemy could not overcome him. God will use the trials and temptations we encounter to pay for a crown of eternal life for us. Although the devil is permitted to approach us, he is not permitted to harm us ultimately. "Blessed is the man who endures temptation; for when he has been approved, he will receive the crown of life which the Lord has promised to those who love Him" (James 1:12).

And so we come to the final temptation of the devil against Jesus. "Again, the devil took Him up on an exceedingly high mountain, and showed Him all the kingdoms of the world and their glory. And he said to Him, 'All these things I will give You if You will fall down and worship me'" (Matthew 4:8–9).

The world was temporarily under the devil's control then, and he declared that if Jesus would bow down and worship him, he would be willing to give it all to Him. Jesus held this in particular importance. He entered the world intending to rescue it, and He is now being given a shortcut to that goal by the devil. The devil offers us many shortcuts to get where God wants us to be, and sometimes we fall prey to that temptation and fail.

"Then Jesus said to him, 'Away with you, Satan! For it is written, 'You shall worship the LORD your God, and Him only you shall serve''" (Matthew 4:10). We can hear echoes of this same temptation later when Satan tries to influence Peter. But Jesus rebuked him, saying, "Get behind Me, Satan! You are an offense to Me, for you are not mindful of the things of God, but the things of men" (Matthew 16:23). The devil believed he could approach Jesus through Peter, but Jesus wouldn't have anything to do with it.

Worship is what's important here, and worshiping the devil rather than God is the enemy's greatest temptation. The devil wanted Jesus to worship him rather than God Almighty, for as the devil said in the book of Isaiah, "I will be like the Most High" (14:14).

The forty days and nights that Jesus spent in prayer played a significant role in His resistance to the devil's temptations in the wilderness. If you have prepared for temptation properly through prayer, temptation cannot harm you; but temptation will undoubtedly be successful if you have not. Jesus foresaw the devil's temptations during the desert experience. The devil didn't know it, but Jesus was ready for anything the devil could throw His way.

Every Christian will face the devil's greatest temptation at some point in their life, even if we can never be certain of the precise day or time. Because of this, it's crucial to be ready, to spend a lot of time in prayer and fellowship with God just like Jesus did. The devil has already tricked you if you believe you are immune to his tricks.

According to the Bible, "angels came and ministered to Him" after this severe temptation in the wilderness (Matthew 4:11). That must have been a wonderful experience, and I would have cherished the opportunity to be there and observe how they cared for Jesus. But the angels serve you and me as Christians in the same way they served our Lord Jesus; we just can't see them. They don't talk to us, and neither do we talk to them, but once we enter heaven, we will learn all about the ministry of angels to Christians.

How I praise You, O God, for protecting me from the enemy of my soul. Help me as I work on my prayer life, so that my prayers will be pleasing to You. Lead me in spiritual warfare that through me You may defeat the enemy. I trust in Your guidance and grace each day. In Jesus' name I pray, amen.

HAVE YOU PRAYED IT THROUGH?

Have you prayed all night, till the break of day,
And the morning light drove the dark away?
Did you linger there, till the morning dew,
In prevailing prayer, did you pray it through?

Did you pray till the answer came,
Did you plead in the Savior's name?
Have you prayed all night till the morning light,
Did you pray till the answer came?

Did you pray it through, till the answer came?
There's a promise true for your faith to claim,
At the place of prayer, Jesus waits for you,
Did you meet Him there, did you pray it through?

As the Master prayed in the garden lone,
Let your prayer be made to the Father's throne,
If you seek His will, He will answer you,
Are you trusting still, have you prayed it through?

William C. Poole (1915)

—16—

STANDING AGAINST THE WILES OF THE DEVIL

Put on the whole armor of God, that you may be able to stand against the wiles of the devil.

Ephesians 6:11

If anyone asked me to choose who in the Bible understood the devil and spiritual warfare best, I would have to go with the apostle Paul. His teaching about spiritual warfare is the most valuable for us today, and he is not just teaching a theory but giving us practical tools based on his own experience. No one faced the enemy and suffered as Paul did.

In the passage quoted above, Paul writes that we have a God-given responsibility as Christians to stand against the devil. Many believers do not expect any spiritual warfare; they think becoming a Christian is the end of the process until they get to heaven. The truth is, if you're a Christian who's alive and walking on this earth, there are many battles to be fought.

I have discovered in my own life that we are often caught up fighting the wrong battles because we have identified the wrong enemy. Some think the enemy is sitting in the pews with them in church or in their family or in their place of employment. But the enemy is spiritual.

In this verse and the verses that follow, Paul points out how important it is for us to comprehend spiritual warfare and how we can prepare for it. Our fight is not casual, nor is it at our discretion. Our enemy, the devil, will attack us at his discretion and on his schedule. But ten thousand enemies cannot stop a praying Christian, or even slow the Christian down, if that person meets their foes with an attitude of complete trust in God. And that's the crucial point to remember regarding spiritual warfare.

Because there are many adversaries in the world, the temptation is to see enemies where none exist. Because we're in conflict with error, we tend to develop a spirit of hostility toward those who disagree with us about anything. Satan cares little whether we go astray after false doctrine or merely turn sour. Either way, he wins.

I believe God's purpose is to give believers ample power to carry the fight to the enemy instead of sitting passively by, allowing the enemy to carry the fight to us. And the best way to keep the enemy out is to keep Christ in. The sheep need not be terrified by the wolf; they must stay close to the Shepherd. But keep in mind that it is not the praying sheep Satan fears, but the presence of the Shepherd. That said, as we move further on and higher up in the Christian life, we may expect to encounter greater difficulties and meet increased hostility from the enemy of our souls.

The apostle Paul gives us this warning: "For we do not wrestle against flesh and blood, but against principalities, against powers, against the rulers of the darkness of this age, against spiritual hosts of wickedness in the heavenly places" (Ephesians 6:12). I wish it were only "flesh and blood" we were wrestling against. If that were the case, education and psychology might prepare us. But Paul insists emphatically that this war is to be fought on a higher plane than that. I admit we have problems with the flesh, and each of us must deal with them, yet our battles must be waged on a much more sophisticated level.

Paul said, "Therefore take up the whole armor of God, that you may be able to withstand in the evil day, and having done all, to stand" (Ephesians 6:13). Notice that Paul says "whole" armor. To stand against the wiles of the devil, we need to be fitted with complete armor for the warfare before us. A partial covering will not work. We must be wholly covered to stand against the devil.

To be ninety-five percent covered leaves five percent vulnerability, and that's all the devil needs. The devil is not concerned about how much we have, but how much we don't have because we don't know when or where the devil will attack. If I am not fully prepared, he will catch me off guard. And that brings me to the point of learning how to trust God.

Paul continues, "Stand therefore, having girded your waist with truth, having put on the breastplate of righteousness, and having shod your feet with the preparation of the gospel of peace" (Ephesians 6:14–15). If we're going to stand against the enemy, we first need to know how to stand before

God. Paul lists three things we need: truth, righteousness, and the gospel. We can't pick two out of the three and expect to live a victorious life before God. We must take and put on everything God has made available to us and stand before Him, completely covered with all that we need to resist the enemy's wiles.

These are not easy things for us to do. Certainly our salvation has been established by Christ, and His grace is free for us. But it's after our salvation is secured that the real battle begins, and that is why we need to be well protected. But if we have what God wants us to have, the devil will never be able to penetrate our lives. Will he try? Of course. But when we stand before God each day, we also must stand against the devil's wiles.

Then Paul said, "Above all, taking the shield of faith with which you will be able to quench all the fiery darts of the wicked one" (Ephesians 6:16). This is so essential. It is our faith that shields us from the enemy's fiery darts.

In 2 Corinthians 5:7, Paul said, "For we walk by faith, not by sight," which means our walk is based on our faith in the Lord Jesus Christ and not on our own understanding. If you look at the life of the apostle Paul, you will see the many times he was in a situation he couldn't explain. I have been in such situations where I didn't know why I was there or even how I would get out of it. In fact, every day of my life, my faith is being tested, and that testing is essential for me to stand against the wiles of the devil. Faith that is passive and inactive lacks wisdom from above and leaves the door open for the devil to manipulate us.

I often think of Jesus' parable of the ten virgins. Five were wise, and five were foolish. If you looked at them, you could not tell the difference. Five got into the kingdom, and five were rejected. They were not rejected because of how they looked or how they talked; they were rejected because they didn't have the oil, the Holy Spirit, in their lives. Our commitment and surrender to the Holy Spirit fuels our faith in God. That comes through the Word of God and by submitting to the Holy Spirit.

As we open God's Word, let us anticipate encountering the Holy Spirit in our obedience. It is the "shield of faith" that will enable us to quench the enemy's fiery darts. For if we are to stand against the enemy, we first need to stand before God. And as we stand before God, we need to meet His requirements when waging war against the devil.

In the book of Revelation, there is a passage concerning the church at Ephesus. Jesus said He loved them but had one thing against them—they had left their first love. They didn't love God as much today as they did a year ago. Essentially, they were growing bored of God, the Bible, worship, and coming together in the fellowship of God's people. This is what's happening today: We are leaving our first love. Because of that, the Church has become vulnerable to enemy attacks. There needs to be a *revival*.

I'm cautious in using that word, but we need to restore in the Church today that passionate love for God that nothing else can satisfy. If you're satisfied with something else, you haven't met the God of the Bible. The more of God you have, the more of God you want.

David said in Psalm 42:1, "As the deer pants for the water brooks, so pants my soul for You, O God." David had a passion for God that could not be satisfied with anything less than God, and he would not stop searching until he found God. His heart panted for God.

In Ephesians 6:17, Paul continues, "And take the helmet of salvation." My salvation is the most important experience I have had in this world, and it changes how I think about everything. The helmet of salvation covers the head, meaning that I need to protect my mind so the world's ideas do not penetrate me and lead me in the wrong direction. So often we are more influenced by our culture's "carnal thinkers" than we are the truth. Thus our minds need to be protected from this influence of the devil.

Finally, the last thing Paul said in the passage just referenced was, "And the sword of the Spirit, which is the word of God." This is essential if we are to stand against the devil's wiles. Our lives must be guided and directed by the Word of God. We must attack the enemy through God's Word, which was exactly what Jesus did when Satan tempted Him in the wilderness. Jesus did not respond theologically, philosophically, or in any other way. Instead, He responded in the way that befitted His nature: "This is what God's Word says. . . ."

I believe we are to do the same. The Bible is not just a collection of stories and lessons to consider. The Bible is a sword, and we must use it to defeat the enemy just as Jesus did in the wilderness.

That may be the end of the armor Paul listed, but I cannot finish there. In Ephesians 6:18, Paul established the spiritual resources we need in our warrior battles: "Praying always with all prayer and supplication in the Spirit, being watchful to this end with all perseverance and supplication for all the saints."

Prayer is the most challenging work the Christian can do. We should be preparing ourselves for the battles before us. We may not know what those battles will be, but we are drawn closer to God in our prayer life. And as we draw closer to God, our lives are influenced by His power and authority.

The devil intends to direct our worship away from God to something else, and it doesn't matter what that is. So if we're going to stand up against the wiles of the enemy, we must commit ourselves to worshiping God, and that begins with our prayer lives.

If we're not worshiping God in our prayers, we're not praying. Every time we pray and worship God, we strengthen our stand against the enemy. Also, when we kneel before God the Father and pray in the name of the Lord Jesus Christ, the Holy Spirit will direct us in our prayers regarding what to pray for and about in accordance with God's will. Let us get to that point where our prayer life becomes saturated with the adoring worship of God.

Heavenly Father, it's a great joy to come into Your presence. My heart is refreshed as I fellowship with You. My days are numbered, my strength is limited, but Your grace makes each day a day of victory. I praise and thank you. In Jesus' name I pray, amen.

WHAT VARIOUS HINDRANCES WE MEET

What various hindrances we meet
in coming to a mercy seat!
Yet who that knows the worth of prayer
but wishes to be often there!

Prayer makes the darkened cloud withdraw,
prayer climbs the ladder Jacob saw;
gives exercise to faith and love,
brings every blessing from above.

Restraining prayer, we cease to fight;
prayer makes the Christian's armor bright;
and Satan trembles when he sees
the weakest saint upon his knees.

While Moses stood with arms spread wide,
success was found on Israel's side;
but when through weariness they failed,
that moment Amalek prevailed.

Have you no words? Ah, think again;
words flow apace when you complain,
and fill your fellow creature's ear
with the sad tale of all your care.

Were half the breath thus vainly spent
to heaven in supplication sent;
your cheerful song would oftener be,
"Hear what the Lord has done for me!"

William Cowper (1779)

A.W. Tozer (1897–1963) was a self-taught theologian, pastor, and writer whose powerful words continue to grip the intellect and stir the soul of today's believer. He authored more than forty books. *The Pursuit of God* and *The Knowledge of the Holy* are considered modern devotional classics. Get Tozer information and quotes at twitter.com/TozerAW.

Reverend James L. Snyder is an award-winning author whose writings have appeared in more than eighty periodicals and fifteen books. He is recognized as an authority on the life and ministry of A.W. Tozer. His first book, *The Life of A.W. Tozer: In Pursuit of God*, won the Readers' Choice Award in 1992 by *Christianity Today*. Because of his thorough knowledge of Tozer, James was given the rights from the A.W. Tozer estate to produce new books derived from over four hundred never-before-published audiotapes. James and his wife live in Ocala, Florida. Learn more at awtozerclassics.com, or contact James at jamessnyder51@gmail.com.